To Love and Work

A Systemic Interlocking of Family, Workplace, and Career

David N. Ulrich, Ph.D.

Harry P. Dunne, Jr., Ph.D.

BRUNNER/MAZEL *Publishers* • New York

Library of Congress Cataloging-in-Publication Data

Ulrich, David N. 1919-
  To love and work.

  Bibliography: p. 195
  Includes index.
  1. Work—Psychological aspects. 2. Family—Mental
health. 3. Family psychotherapy. I. Dunne, Harry P.,
1942-   . II. Title. [DNLM: 1. Family. 2. Family
Therapy. 3. Love. 4. Work. BF 481 U45t]
RC488.5.U47 1986   616.89'156   86-6798
ISBN 0-87630-421-8

Published by
BRUNNER/MAZEL, INC.
19 Union Square West
New York, New York 10003

Dedicated to Judy and Mary Lou

Contents

Acknowledgments

The concepts on which this book is based derive primarily from the approach of Ivan Boszormenyi-Nagy to the treatment of people in families. In the years since receiving Dr. Boszormenyi-Nagy's tutelage, the senior author has had a growing awareness of the debt owed to his genius, a realization shared by colleagues and students. At the same time, we owe it to Dr. Boszormenyi-Nagy to make it clear that while this book reflects his influence, we do not present it as a statement of his thinking.

We are also in debt to Thomas Fogarty, whose brilliant interpretations of Murray Bowen's theories provided the junior author with a mode of approach to family therapy. The two authors have carried on a dialogue for the past several years on the subject of how the theories of Boszormenyi-Nagy relate to those of Bowen. Out of this dialogue has emerged a frame of reference in which the concepts of Boszormenyi-Nagy and Bowen are seen as complementary, an approach that, we believe, has proven to have synergistic value.

We extend a very special kind of acknowledgment to our colleague Carol Peschke, who was very much a part of the inception of this book, and whose insights and ideas, generated from the perspective of a career counselor who has guided many people along the tortuous path of career development, played a major part in getting this project under way.

We also wish to acknowledge our deep indebtedness to those individuals without whom this book could not exist, the clients who graciously and courageously agreed to make their experiences available to others.

Introduction

The person who wants to speak with his or her "own voice" in the workplace may be constrained not only by the requirements of the workplace and by the effort to balance the present demands of work and family, but most of all by family voices from the past that direct, goad, or restrain. These messages of designation, which continue to direct how one should function, exert a claim that may be antithetical to the claim coming from within the self, yet one continues to be attached to them out of love, loyalty, and concern. Freud said that to be healthy, we must be able to love and work, yet it appears that the demands of love and of work often clash.

It has become clear enough that in contemporary society the individual must be able to balance the demands of the family system and the work system in a kind of mental ledger that may not even be consciously maintained. While moving back and forth, working within and between these systems, the person also looks for what we call a "zone of spontaneity," a space in which one is able to speak with one's "own voice," to perform and produce as one sees fit rather than solely according to the cues of a parent or supervisor. A designation is fortunate when it includes the encouragement to act upon one's own strivings, provided this does not become a command. But we have found that people are often confined by invisible parameters whose design is the work of generations. Sometimes the parameters are so loose that they are unimportant, sometimes so binding that they govern strictly the course of a lifetime's effort.

We refer to the parameters as "invisible" because it seems that they often impose their effects without people's being aware that they exist at all. The parameters are set by a process in which a multitude of factors combine to establish what we have chosen to call a designation of what the person is to do in life and how he or she is to do it. These factors include such realities as sibling rank and spacing, intellectual endowment, and the financial status of the family; the narcissistic needs of the parents who may, for example, want children as caretakers; and the mandates laid down by past generations of family members concerning what new members of this family are to be, to do, and to stand for. While children may accept their designated place out of fear of being left with no place at all, the principal holding power of designation comes from the child's loyalty, his or her sense of what is owed in exchange for having received life and nurture. This often leads even young children (perhaps much younger than Freud ever imagined) to put concern for family ahead of concern for self, a process that may mean never-ending payments on an undefinable debt.

We have encountered a vast range of messages of designation. For example, "Succeed like your father," "Fail like your father," "Succeed where your father failed," "Succeed and fail," "Defer to your brother," "Take care of your mother," "It's dangerous out there, keep your head down," "There's a lot out there—if you want it, go for it."

We realize that for people unaccustomed to working with the multigenerational aspects of family systems, the notion of adults being bound by designations laid down for them in their childhood, the notion that grandma may have something to do with how you respond to your boss, may seem absurd. To us it is no more absurd than the notion that your mortgage payment is due every month. The mortgage may be an old document, but if you forget about it the bank will remind you, and in many cases this is how the grown child perceives the demands of family designations.

The holding power of designation comes out of one's family loyalties, but that is only part of the story. The other part is the remarkable synergistic effect of the terms of designation and the terms by which everything proceeds in the workplace. Businesses are not organized like families and bosses cannot function like mothers or fathers; it is counterproductive to blur these distinctions. But much of what goes on at work does bear resemblance to what occurs in the family. Businesses have to be organized in vertical hierarchies, with their pattern of bosses and subordinates. Upon this basic template, it is inevitable that the emotional patterns of the vertical family structure will get superimposed. When the boss speaks, it may seem like father or mother speaking, and the regressive transference phenomena thus activated may go well beyond the transference one person puts upon another; within the individual, the sense of being inside the family system can get reactivated. But one does not even have to wait for the boss to speak; it is by now well recognized that when an employee enters the workplace, the family baggage does not get checked at the door. The old patterns of attitude and action are ready to be called up, and it is remarkable how easily one can find actors at work who are ready and willing to stand in for the missing family members. It seems as if no matter how much attention is given to "human resources management," the way people actually behave at work cannot be accounted for by the needs of the business itself. Instead, the workplace is actively conducive to the playing out of designations.

The ubiquitous operations of triangles aid and abet this playing out. Triangles carry the multigenerational messages within the family, and likewise they carry the multilevel messages within the workplace. Triangles seem to be pernicious; they tend to facilitate the transmission of stress downwards and block communication upwards. The way people move about within triangles at work, as at home, gets a significant impetus from the forces of designation.

The vertical structure of the family has been conceptualized as a dimension of past time, i.e., stretching back through the generations. Inevitably the vertical dimension at work will be perceived in the same way, i.e., the bosses stand for prior generations, past values, and established procedures. In contrast, we conceptualize productivity as something that occurs in the dimension of present time, the here and now, calling upon people for the kind of spontaneous innovation whose essence is freedom from past dictates. The tension between old and new ways of doing things at work parallels the tension in the family between the old mandates and the new strivings of the individual to find his or her "own voice."

It has long been recognized that the nonhierarchical, semi-autonomous work group can be a key to improved productivity. This is essentially a group of peers, and we believe it is significant that this structure has no parallel within the family system. The work group does not, for instance, give automatic recognition to rank by chronological age, as does the sibling structure. The work group, in other words, does not provide any handy pegs on which to hang the family baggage. We think this is a clue to its effectiveness.

The interaction between family process and work is by no means a one-way street; not only do designations have an impact on what occurs in the workplace, but what happens at work significantly influences what goes on in the family. One of the major influences may occur through displacement; e.g., frustrations encountered during the day at work or major frustrations encountered over time with one's career may present themselves as marital conflict or parent-child conflict, and such a displacement may stubbornly resist efforts at its dispersal.

The impact of work on the family is of crucial significance in another respect. Work has been conceptualized as one of the three factors basic to one's separation from the family of origin—individuation and the formation of peer relationships being the other two (McGoldrick & Carter, 1982). As we see it, work does not simply provide the funds for separation; it is also the process whereby one earns the right to move beyond one's designated function and to perform as one chooses—this is the very essence of individuation.

This process is characterized by tension among family members. From the time the person initiates his or her first exploratory moves toward his or her own way of doing things, whether this is how to tie shoes or prepare homework, there will be tension between the person and the family over questions of how things should be done. As stated earlier, many influences reinforce this tension, including the parents' own narcissistic needs and concerns, such as their anxiety about their own approaching obsolescence.

As we see it, becoming individuated means escaping the bonds of designation, stepping outside the triangles in which the tensions over how to perform are generated, and being able to approach others at work with an open mind. This does not mean laying aside self-interest; it does not rule out playing hardball with the competition. But it does mean, for example, that the person can function as manager without a constant compulsion to enforce the dictates of the vertical hierarchy. The person may, in other words, become a facilitator, enabling others to perform, a role that can have the utmost significance for the business even though in general it seems to receive relatively little recognition or reward.

The process of individuation does not follow some preordained "natural course of events." Just as there may be competition at work, there may be collisions at home and between work and home, as the legitimate interests of spouses and children are thrown into competition with one another for available time and resources. To make life livable, "yield" and "squeeze" points have to be recognized and continual negotiations have to take place so that things will come out reasonably fair. Individuation means being able to master a balancing act, keeping all of the competing demands and expectations that arise within the work system, the family system, and between these two systems in a relative state of balance. This becomes especially true when both parents work and must balance their needs as individuals and as a couple, against the demands of job and children.

The fact that work is a crucial component of life for individuals and families means that it should be, but rather seldom is, regarded as a crucial component of therapy. The nature of one's sense of self is such that an insult received or an impediment encountered in one area of life can readily cause a reaction or disturbance in the other. A wife who comes to therapy because she is convinced her husband is having an affair may be substituting this issue for the unfaced reality that he has suffered a possibly irreversible depression following failure at work. A husband who rails at his wife over the quality of her housework may be substituting this issue for his conflicts about work. To take it at face value that the couple is undergoing a marital conflict may be to miss the core of their difficulties. A mother who brings a complaint about her daughter's academic performance may be using this as a thin veneer over a mother-daughter rivalry that is exacerbated by the husband's withdrawal from the family. The focus of conflict can move instantaneously from work to personal relationships and back again.

In our view, the therapeutic task of breaking the bonds of designation and moving along the path toward individuation and freedom of choice can be accomplished only by a process of identifying and acknowledging the *legitimate* claims imposed by one's origins, as a precursor to discarding those claims that have lost their legitimacy or relevance. Without this acknowledgment of one's origins, the attempt to establish one's own position in the here-and-now is likely to be void of meaning. This process is one that calls for dialogue, either the attempt at actual dialogue with those participants in one's origins who are still living, or at least the effort to think through what this dialogue might have been. The dialogue, real or imaginary, is a kind of negotiation about what one owes to and is owed by the family. This negotiation is the same in principle as that which one carries on with one's contemporaries at work and at home, in order to arrive at a fair balancing of interests.

References to "family baggage carried into the workplace" should not be taken to mean that we believe family process is *bad*. Rather, we are looking at what occurs when patterns that govern the family, for better or for worse, inevitably, and often counterproductively, are carried over into the workplace.

To Love and Work

A Systemic Interlocking of Family, Workplace, and Career

1

Two Worlds Conjoined

When people talk about their jobs and their family life, it sometimes sounds as if they are struggling to occupy two different worlds. Some mention a kind of magic moment they experience during their trip to work—in the car or on the bus or train—when they step out of their family persona and take on a somewhat different "self." And eight, nine, or ten hours later, during their return trip or through the enactment of some day's-end ritual—changing clothes, reading the mail—they try to leave their workplace persona behind in order to resume the role of husband or wife, father or mother. But regardless of how they strive to "leave the job at the office," they carry home with them a variety of emotions and issues which impact on family roles and family transactions.

At the same time, all members of an organization are plugged into a family system that has an impact on their behavior at work. And hard as they might try to leave the family behind, they bring with them into the workplace specific attitudes, values, emotions, patterns of actions, expectations, legacies, loyalties, and communication styles that are indigenous to the family system. Family dynamics from the past, as well as those from the present, have a dramatic impact not only on the career issues faced by each individual but upon the work setting as well. One person's family legacy mandating success or failure, for example, will have a crucial impact on his or her career and, less obviously, on the workplace itself, with repercussions for other individuals and other families. In other words, each person who works is engaged at some level in a delicate balancing act which, performed successfully, can generate autonomy and integrity for the individual both as a worker and as family member. But should the balancing act fail, complications ensue. For instance, when the family exerts stress on an executive, as Kathy Wiseman (1982) has pointed out, the executive is more vulnerable to organizational stress. And since the converse is true as well, it is easy to see how the family and the workplace can squeeze the worker between them.

That workplace and family dynamics are synergistically linked is a fact of modern life, with implications for vocational counselors and human resources personnel as well as psychotherapists. The workplace is alive with issues that have special meaning for therapists, especially those with a systems awareness. Interlocking triangles complicate the most simple transactions. Multigenerational issues, symbolic or all too real, play themselves out in larger-than-life proportions. Interpersonal dealings that build or diminish levels of relational trustworthiness between individuals or within groups are readily observable. The work environment, organizational efficiency, and even the almighty bottom line can be profoundly affected by the systemic transactions that are certain to evolve in every setting where human beings interact.

For some, of course, the workplace serves as a haven from the stress, disappointment, frustration, and confusion encountered in the family; for others the family serves as a place where the wounds inflicted in ''that jungle out there'' can be soothed. But either way, the dual existence can cause difficulties in terms of integration and balance for both the individual and the two demanding systems—workplace and family—in which he or she lives.

Therapists often unwittingly reinforce this duality during assessment and therapy by failing to give due regard to the impact of the workplace on the family and to the worker's efforts to balance what he or she owes, gives, and takes in each of these settings. It is common practice, of course, to inquire about a client's job, but all too often therapists assume either that the true dynamics of the workplace are beyond their area of impact, or worse, that they understand those dynamics and the work context once a label has been offered regarding the client's job; "I'm a salesman for Bendix," gets filed away as if the phrase actually held some definitive, personal meaning. Except in cases where workplace or career issues are directly involved in the presenting problem, the impact of the family system on the workplace and of the work system on the family are often set aside as the therapist attends to more pressing, and perhaps what seem to be more clinically relevant, concerns. Even when a client raises career issues, therapists frequently view them only as symptomatic.

It seems ironic that a setting in which a person spends the majority of his or her waking hours would be given only passing consideration by a professional attempting to understand that person's life.

Therapists gain considerable therapeutic leverage by paying explicit attention to the connections between work and the family and by assessing ways in which the family's demands, both past and present, have affected the individual's efforts toward a definition of productive striving. And we have come to believe that if work-related or career issues do not emerge as a significant feature of the presenting problem, they should be explored at the therapist's initiative, something that almost never happens in standard psychoanalytic practice and rarely in practices based upon the family systems approaches. Indeed, the tension between the family's designation of the child's usefulness and the child's own definitions of productive effort—and the subsequent impact of this tension on career choice and work experiences— may be one of the most critical aspects of an individual's developmental history. In addition, the family system itself can be better understood if attention is paid to work-related experience, attitudes, and values. Viewed in this light, the family of origin comes more fully to life, taking on a new dimension that adds depth to other aspects of life. People in the client's past, even those who are long dead, begin to seem more real, and when accounts of their working lives are examined their ambitions, dreams, and fears seem more tangible.

Career issues are too frequently viewed by psychotherapists as belonging to somebody else's turf and patients are invited to take their work-related concerns to a specialist, the career counselor. But if most psychotherapists handicap themselves by overlooking the importance of career and workplace issues, the traditional career counselor is hampered that much more by the tendency to avoid anything that is too deeply personal, most notably the impact of the family.

THE CASE OF MARK

A few years ago at the request of a client, one of the authors attended a brainstorming session with a career counselor in order to add clinical considerations to the issues that had emerged from a battery of vocational interest and aptitude tests the counselor had administered. During the session the family therapist spoke about significant themes that had emerged in his client's family history and pointed out ways these themes clarified or altered the interpretations of the career counselor. He spoke of triangles and legacies, entitlement and loyalty, repeating patterns of relationship and degree of individuation. In turn, the career counselor suggested areas where test data added depth or even pointed out new directions for therapy. And after the session, as the therapist and counselor were shaking hands by the elevator, the therapist expressed his admiration for the thoroughness of the counselor's data, but said he did not see how the counselor could get the full picture without taking a look at the family. And the counselor responded that he had never been able to figure out how therapists ever really knew their patients without work history and aptitude data.

Mark, the subject of this brainstorming session, was the 44-year-old stepfather of a child-centered family that had been in family therapy for nearly a year. He and his wife had both been previously married, and in addition to the two stepchildren who lived with him, Mark had two children living in another state with his ex-wife and her new husband.

One night after a family therapy session, Mark mentioned almost as an afterthought that he had been having "a little trouble down at work."

"Oh?" said the therapist. "Well, you hide it well."

During the session Mark had functioned in his usual role as the voice of self-assured reason, offering his observations as an involved, caring, yet more objective adult and employing his remarkable ability to understand both sides of the conflict that alternately simmered and raged between his wife and one of his stepchildren. The only thing the therapist knew about Mark's job was that he was a successful executive with a Fortune 500 corporation and that in compensation for whatever it was he did as an assistant director, he was rewarded with a six-figure income. Indeed, Mark seemed most unusual to the therapist who was accustomed to dealing with hard-driven, disengaged, sealed-over, and unavailable representatives of the business community. In contrast, Mark had been appropriately supportive to everyone, not only during family therapy sessions, but at home as well. He was able to tap into and express his feelings and use these to let his wife and stepchildren know where they stood with him and what they could and could not expect. In addition, he readily grasped elusive systems concepts such as loyalty, legacy, triangles, and emotional movement, and often helped the therapist by providing family anecdotal material that brought these concepts to life. The focus of therapy had remained on the problematic triangle formed by Mark's wife, her ex-husband, and the identified patient, a teenage daughter; and by the time Mark dropped his comment about having "a little trouble down at work," his wife had taken successful steps to solidify her coparenting relationship with her ex-husband.

It turned out that Mark's career problems weren't as simple or minor as he had made them sound. In a word, Mark was being fired, although at his level the word "termination" with its more refined implications was used.

For more than a year, Mark explained during the next family

session, he had only been "going through the motions" at work. "My job is a job," he said, "only minimally satisfying. More and more I feel like a hollow man. I want to deal on a deeper level with people. I want to be challenged and be in a position to make a difference, achieve something special. I have important responsibilities but I want more out of work than I get, which is a lot of work but little challenge and little I ever see as worthwhile." His last promotion had forced him to delegate every aspect of his job that held any real interest for him, he reported, but he quickly added that his lack of drive had predated this promotion.

Mark's apathy had been mentioned by superiors in performance reviews and in several painful confrontations, but these did nothing to put Mark back on track. Finally Mark's boss told him that his future with the firm looked grim, citing, in addition to Mark's attitude, that he was too laborious in getting from point "A" to point "B," giving too much attention to nonessential details and to time-consuming planning. Also mentioned was Mark's tendency to either overmanage or undermanage his subordinates or at times to become too involved in their personal lives. "Maybe," his boss told him, "you'd be better off at a smaller company."

"What do you make of this business with your subordinates?" the therapist asked Mark.

"Oh, it's true," he said. "I'm the company social worker."

"It's the same thing he does in the family," his teenage stepdaughter said. "It makes him feel important."

Mark laughed and said that he guessed it was true. He seemed to be forever protecting people, explaining one guy to the other, settling conflicts, making peace, buffering the weak from harm. "Down at work recently I've been protecting Ben, a minority employee, and Allen, an older man, from any close scrutiny," Mark said. "I guess it makes me feel like I'm doing something for somebody. But my efforts sure as hell aren't appreciated up above."

As part of their executive outplacement package, Mark's company had offered to underwrite career counseling services, so Mark spared no expense in his efforts to understand his interests, aptitudes, and, most important of all, his attitude change. He worked with a leader in the field to explore "patterns of success" and to take test batteries that matched his values, attitudes, and personal preferences against those of sample populations from various career areas. He emerged from this consultation with a better understanding of his interests, but something still seemed to be missing, so he went for a consultation with a firm famous for its in-depth assessment of aptitudes and knowledge. He took tests that measured his inductive and analytical reasoning, spatial and nonspatial thinking, personality (in objective and subjective terms), pitch discrimination, tonal memory, rhythm memory, ability to observe and remember numbers, words, details, design patterns, and objects, graphoria (paper-and-pencil tests measuring speed and accuracy), ideaphoria (rate of idea generation), verbal and mathematical vocabularies, color vision, and even dexterity with tweezers.

Mark requested an individual session with the family therapist to discuss his career problem and he came armed with enough printed material to fill a book, all of it impressive in its content and attention to detail. The trouble was that it left Mark more paralyzed than when he started his exploration. Before the analysis he was simply stuck in a job that bored him; now he realized that his interests and values stood in opposition to his aptitudes and skills.

It was not as black and white as that, but after hearing the results of his testing, this was how Mark felt. The tests indicated that he valued aesthetic achievement and helping people above all other goals, and yet his education and the career ladder he had climbed included neither of these.

"I seem to be a subjective person who functions better at objective tasks," he said. He had scored low in idea generation and high in memory function and visual discrimination. "The tests show that I'm good at putting facts and figures together and synthesizing," Mark said. "Precisely what I do now. Trouble is, I don't enjoy it because I'd rather be doing something creative or artistic." But the tests said he was not creative. He understood concepts quickly, and once given a model he could add detail and interpret in creative ways:

Mark: I'm not one of those guys who can structure from nothing, but I can pull preexisting pieces together and make something out of them. I probably should have been a recording engineer or something like that, twisting dials while somebody else makes the music.

Therapist: Does any of this remind you of anyone?

Mark: Dad. It's Dad all over again. He's a behind-the-scenes detail man and so am I.

Therapist: And who gave you your need to help people? Mother?

Mark: No. I'm sure I get my appreciation for poetry and music and art from her. My need to help probably comes from the role I played in my family. I was the helper and explainer for so many years that I just got comfortable with it.

Naturally, Mark was frightened by the prospect of being compelled to start over again at 44, giving up the salary and perks of his elevated position and retraining himself for something new. At the same time, as far as he could see, there did not seem to be any way out of his bind; like most of us, Mark was equally attached to both his aptitudes and his interests, even though they did not coincide. This was shaping up to be one of the toughest tests he would ever have to face.

Mark had been exposed to enough family systems thinking to be readily open to the suggestion that his impasse might have its roots in his family of origin. And it did not take long before the standoff represented by the clash between his aptitudes and interests was recognized as an accurate representation of the standoff that he felt had existed throughout his childhood between his parents. Mark's mother, with whom he had been overly close until her death, was a "warm, sensitive soul who spent a great deal of time alone in museums—sort of a displaced European aristocrat." She had instilled in Mark an appreciation for "life's finer things," and from the time he was very young she had insisted that he was uniquely gifted and destined to make a special contribution to the world. His father was a more earthy sort, harsh, demanding, and distant. "He's always been more comfortable with objects than people, and at times he could be a real dictatorial son-of-a-bitch." According to Mark, his mother and father had little in common other than their son, who some-how had the ability to get along well (at least superficially, in his father's case) with them both. He was anxious to please his mother and took every opportunity to display sensitivities and talents that were in keeping with her interests. At the same time, though, he was anxious to win his father's approval and worked hard beside him on tasks and projects around the house, often displaying a unique aptitude for the work, and, in spite of himself, rather enjoying it. In school, he found that detail work in math and the sciences came naturally to him while he had to struggle with the more "artsy" courses such as literature and music. In short, Mark seemed to have his father's aptitudes and his mother's interests.

"I felt all alone when I was a kid," Mark said, trying to tell the therapist what it had been like in his family. "And it seems like I took all the blame."

Further exploration revealed that Mark had served as the family lightning rod, drawing his father's anger away from his mother and his mother's loneliness away from his father. The triangle was classic. His mother would move toward her son in response to her alienation from his father. "She needed to have her interests in art, music, and literature shared so that these sides of herself were valued," Mark said, "and Dad couldn't or wouldn't give her that." His father, who had a strong need for validation from his wife, would feel the distance and sense the special relationship between mother and son, so he would move toward his wife with harsh demands and criticism, in keeping with his style for managing closeness. At this point Mark would take steps to draw his father's anger upon himself. Over time Mark had shifted back and forth between an overly close, smothering relationship with his mother and a conflicted, angry closeness with his father, until his teen years when he began to seek distance by reaching outside the family. During that phase, when Mark began to establish relationships with peers, especially females, his mother would move in with strong disapproval, causing Mark to try to regain her approval through renewed, intensified involvement in their shared interests.

As an adult, Mark had always had a sense of being in two

worlds at once, a self-contradictory duality. "I can never seem to win," he said, and that reflected his family past. If he pursued his own emerging interests or drew close to his father through shared activity, his mother felt betrayed, as if Mark's choice were to reject her. So he usually ended up in a frenzy of activity aimed at pleasing both his parents—a father who might have been pleased had Mark managed to come up with the right performance in the right area at the right time, and a mother who was pleased simply by what Mark was, as long as he showed himself to be what she needed him to be. Later, when this triangle was recapitulated at work and at home, Mark would again enter a frenzy of activity.

A less obvious recapitulation of the primary family triangle had also reached out over time to influence Mark's career. While married to his former wife, Mark's career had flourished and he had been a "fast-tracker," ascending the corporate ladder several rungs at a time. "My marriage was a disaster," he said, "but at work I was a hero and I ate up the approval." In a triangle involving wife and work (personified by his boss), Mark had duplicated that family moment when he moved away from his mother and connected with his father in the use of his more natural abilities. But this was to change dramatically when he married his present wife, a woman who valued his more sensitive, "human" qualities more than she did his abilities or achievements. The configuration of the triangle shifted, just as it had with disconcerting regularity while Mark was growing up, so that now the work-wife-self triangle became a recapitulation of that family moment when Mark drew close to his mother through shared interests and stood at a resentful distance from his father. No wonder Mark's emotional response to the prospect of leaving his job was similar to the feeling that came when he finally decided to leave his first wife. "I felt both peaceful and melancholy," he said.

As therapy progressed, Mark explored other connections between his career difficulties and his family history; his need to be seen as unique and special was given attention. Mark came to realize,

I have been approaching my boss and my peers with a need to be defined by them, and I've been putting a big chunk of me on the table when I do, so that I see a lack of responsiveness from them as not only a misunderstanding of the problem but also as a rejection of me—my uniqueness. Not only am I looking to be defined but also acknowledged as unique, the way I was at home. I get that from my wife, but not due to assets and characteristics I feel good about. At work, it's more like Dad and all his demands and his finger-pointing.

His mother's expectations were incredibly compelling. "Her faith in me was overwhelming," Mark said, "her belief that I'm so unique that I will in some way leave my mark on the world." This put him under an impossible designation, a mandate that left him feeling like a failure regardless of how high he climbed on the company ladder because the corporation was not the place where one might make beautiful music or write something that would last. "If not a poem then the analysis of a poem." No wonder the more mundane aspects of his job left him feeling numb.

In an effort to explore and reframe Mark's legacy, the therapist had Mark make a list of what he viewed as the interests, abilities, and values of both his parents. He was then directed to go over this list with his father and invite his father to generate a similar list of his own, a process that caused Mark to eventually develop a different picture of his parents and their compatibility. It turned out that in actuality his mother and father met on firmer common ground than he had realized, with more shared interests than they had displayed to him. And Mark began to see that their different interests and skills "didn't contradict each other as much as they complemented each other."

What had caused Mark to perceive his mother and father as opposites throughout his life was the fact that any move he made toward one of them was perceived as his having forsaken the other. The inventories he made with the therapist's support led him to discover that in reality the differences between his parents were bridgeable and that he could now act without fear to find a synthesis. As this therapeutic work progressed, Mark and his supervisor at work began to notice a change in his attitude and his approach. Mark came to see the trouble he had been having on the job as an opportunity to grow and move into a position that more fully reflected his interests, and eventually the job that was about to evaporate took on added importance. At the same time, Mark intensified his involvement with his church as a way of satisfying his need to work with and help people. A year after Mark had been told that his future looked grim, a major promotion came his way, making a career change unnecessary.

As was clear in Mark's case, the family system, where the personality is shaped, forges our attitudes relating to performance and productive striving. Work-related themes reach back into the family history to a time when the child's usefulness within the family was defined. For most, this process of defined usefulness has had a substantial bearing on the process of identity formation and individuation and has profoundly shaped the individual's attitudes toward work performance. An individual's approach to work then, cannot be fully understood without attention to family systems, past and present. Conversely, the individual can be better understood through an examination of attitudes, values, and approaches to work.

"What do you want to be when you grow up?" asked innocently enough of most children, contains the implication that "you are what you do." And for most adults, work remains our best way to present ourselves to the world. Faced with the question "Who are you?" most of us will talk about what we do, as if our career labels and job descriptions might actually help define us.

Until work begins the individual cannot fully realize the goals of adulthood: establishing a marriage, starting a family, acquiring buying power for the essentials and some of the good things in life. Genuine autonomy is all but impossible without financial self-support, so in this sense, work provides leverage for individuation-separation to occur. But the connection between work and the individuation-separation process goes far deeper, and is of greater clinical relevance than the question of having dollars in one's pocket.

2

The Tension Between the Individual and the Family

THE ISSUE OF BEING USEFUL

An individual's passage through the life cycle shows the effects of tension between the kinds of usefulness the family designates for the person and the kinds of productive striving the person seeks for him- or herself. The small child begins to move toward individuation and separation, gradually shifting to awareness of him- or herself as a separate person. Much later efforts to separate involve such issues as making one's own decisions, living apart, and seeking a sense of validation of the self through relationships and work. One person may go at these tasks quite vigorously; another may seem so passive that the movement can scarcely be discerned. Regardless of the individual approach to separation, there tends to be a pull away from the power of the family to impose its expectations.

There will probably be both restricting and liberating elements in the efforts of the family to define how the person can be useful. Whatever encourages the child to develop his or her initiative toward some productive outcome may be considered liberating. For example, the small child may be encouraged to dress and wash without help, put toys away, start using crayons, and so

15

on. It may also be liberating if, while stressing the child's responsibility to the family, the parents make it clear that this is done
in preparation for assuming later responsibilities outside the
family.

Conversely, anything that attaches rigid priority to the child's
service to the family will usually be restrictive. Openly or covertly
the parents and siblings may hold the parameters of the child's
functioning within the narrow range defined by the family's
needs. In a multiple-family group session, a parent was complaining about how her teenage son had changed. Asked how she
wanted her son to be, she replied, "I would like him to be
younger." Being younger, although obviously impossible and
a desire not in the son's best interest, would force him to remain
within the space allocated to him by the family. Or a family's
overt emphasis may be put on how the child may develop in
order to enhance his or her ultimate usefulness outside the family, yet the covert intent may have more to do with the family's
needs than with the needs of the child or of the outside world.

The way the family of origin copes with the move of the individual toward separation will have a profound bearing on how
the person handles all later events having to do with work and
family. As was spelled out in the Introduction, the focus of this
book is on how individuals move back and forth between the
work and family systems, how each system affects the way the
person functions in the other system, and how the person may
seek to achieve balance between the systems and still step back
far enough from their combined effects to preserve a zone of
spontaneous functioning. This achievement of balance can be arrived at only through a process of *negotiation* and will be affected
by how earlier negotiations went between the family and the
child. The person who was enabled successfully to handle the
negotiations in the family will, for instance, be more likely to
generate his or her own definitions of how to be most productive at work, in contrast to letting the definition of usefulness
emerge from the cues of a supervisor.

In their formulations concerning the life cycle, McGoldrick and
Carter (1982) suggest that the separation process depends on
three essential factors: individuation, formation of peer relation-

ships, and work. We propose that the issue of the child's usefulness, i.e., what the child is to do and how he or she is to do it, may, in our culture at least, have become the hub of the process of individuation. It is here, perhaps more than in any other part of one's life, that differences between the family and child come to exist, be recognized, and developed.

The process we are describing permeates our lives and is heavily overdetermined; i.e., all kinds of psychological and transactional factors within the family will be brought to bear, sometimes under great pressure, upon the child's performance. The infant's rhythms of excitation may not coincide with the mothering adult's availability. The child's idea of how to tie a shoe may be different from the parent's, who may want it done more neatly, more quietly, or without long pauses for contemplating bugs. The child may want to pack the school bag at night; the parent may demand that the child get to bed and pack the schoolbag in the morning. Packing the bag at night may mean getting to stay up later; the desire for greater autonomy that is implicit here may conflict with the mother's wish to have more uninterrupted evening time with the father. When it comes to homework, use of tools, or use of athletic gear, the parents and siblings may withhold help, smother the child with help, or give help that may be permeated with tension resulting from some family member's ambivalence about permitting this child to achieve. Or, the other family members may give enough help so that the child can proceed without too much discomfort.

The constitutional differences among family members may set up tensions; e.g., the child may be smarter or not as smart; more skillful or less; more artistic or less. One child may engage lustily in screaming back at the mother while a sibling, presented with the same stimulus, may run for cover.

On a wide front, including studies, athletics, music, art, hobbies, use of tools, etc., the attitudes of parents and siblings, which may have been determined by a great many factors that have little or nothing to do with the child's own unique qualities, will exert the most intense impact on the child, whether supporting, coercing, or prohibiting. Among these factors, legacy is often the most powerful. The family's attitudes toward awards, prizes, trophies, and honor grades can shape the child's emerging view of what he or she should invest with meaning. The child will quickly sense and internalize, for example, a parent's attitude that nothing else counts compared to getting to the top, or that whenever you do something good, something bad will come along to balance it.

The impact will be especially powerful if the child has consciously or unconsciously chosen the activity because it provides an opportunity to differentiate from siblings and parents.

Further issues will arise as the child progresses through adolescence: whether to attend college, and where, what courses to take, whether to transfer or drop out for a year and work. All of these choices, of course, may have very different meanings for the growing child than for the parents or siblings. The tradition-bound parent, still very much with us, is horrified at, and very hostile about, the child's choice of Harvard in a family of Yale graduates. Or who says, "Forget about writing; you have to earn a living." Or who is stunned at the child's suggestion that he or she might like to join an ashram. Or who says, simply enough, "Forget it, you will never amount to anything." The child, in turn, may be using the expressed preference for a school or occupation, not so much because of any intrinsic interest, but as a way of probing whether the parent will or will not tolerate any deviation from existing family values. If the permission to deviate is given, the child's interest in the particular choice may be short-lived. Or the child may come to realize something that until now has seemed most improbable: that while the parent will always view the matter differently, this does not have to be catastrophic because the parent and the child are both entitled to their own point of view.

THE QUALITY OF NEGOTIATION

These differences between family and the growing child may merely provide stimulating talk at the dinner table or they can flare into serious conflicts of beliefs and values that may concern the choice of activities, the way the activity is to be carried out, or both. From beneath the surface, long-standing but unrecognized, or not yet acknowledged, expectations can suddenly emerge. The full force of old family legacies can be felt for the first time, as when the father says to the daughter, ''It is not worth sending you to college.''

The quality of the negotiations between the family and the individual about what he or she intends to do and how these goals, whether short- or long-term, are to be pursued, can influence nuances of a person's later functioning in ways that are scarcely discernible; for instance, a person may go through his or her working life with a vague sense of discomfort and apprehension about presenting ideas to superiors, as a result of how ideas were treated at the family dinner table. The importance of what was said, how it was said, and what was left unsaid (or should have been) can linger over the years, with long-range effects that are anything but subtle. As Schein (1978) put it from the perspective of an organizational consultant, personality styles learned in childhood continue to operate throughout life, and old coping styles tend to be reactivated during major life transitions. We would add that old coping styles can be reactivated under almost any major kind of stress, and that two kinds of coping are involved here: being able to perform and being able to negotiate, first with family and later with others, in order to perform in accordance with one's own ability, style, and preference. This intricate negotiation process shapes the individual's approach to productive effort.

The interplay between the claims of the family and the emerging efforts of a daughter to strive for herself will become apparent in the case of Roberta.*

---

*In order to ensure that the origins of these clinical materials will be adequately disguised, this case is presented as a composite of several cases, the dynamics of which are quite similar. Most of our cases are not composite. The ones that are will be identified. These and other clinical materials were obtained from notes made during interviews. Most of the quotations are paraphrases of what our clients actually said, while occasional longer passages are verbatim transcripts of tapes. So while we cannot vouch for the literal accuracy of our dialogues as presented, we believe we have been true to the essence of what our clients were telling us.

THE DROPOUT

Roberta, 24, was referred for family therapy because her individual therapist recognized that one-to-one treatment was not getting to the core of the problem. At the time of the referral from individual to family therapy, Roberta had returned to live at home with her parents and three younger siblings, having dropped out of art school in another city during the first semester. Presenting symptoms were depression and confusion about life goals.

In their first session, the family enthusiastically agreed that Roberta had a great deal of talent and described how they had encouraged her to study. Roberta said the school had expected more than she could deliver and she had gotten "spaced out" from trying. Anxiety finally took over to such an extent that she was unable to study at all. She could not think about the future because she was not sure of being good enough to compete. The school staff gave lavish praise for her work, but people had always done that so it seemed ordinary, and it made her feel like a fake. So, paradoxically, when praised by a staff member she would find herself freezing up. Finally, she began to wonder if she had picked the school just to get away from home.

In subsequent family sessions the therapist observed that Roberta's father was highly authoritarian, giving out directives in a derogatory style to his wife and younger children, while Roberta pounced on everything he said. Her father encouraged this, on the grounds that having a good argument with your father was a good way to prepare for life. "Come practice on me," was his message. But she could sense that her assaults actually left him hurt and defensive. Far from helping Roberta open life's door, her father seemed to be crumpling across the threshold.

In response, the family therapist tried to build the father-daughter relationship till the father could cease to feel so isolated and abandoned, till he could begin to relinquish his tyranny. With the therapist's coaching, Roberta became less confrontational and more caring, and her father indeed seemed to relax. What Roberta had been searching for seemed to be coming to pass. But what looked like progress in the sessions was not being matched by progress outside. Before long Roberta was hinting at suicide. ''I'm working so hard, but they won't change. It's not worth it.''

On reappraising the situation, the therapist realized that Roberta was either trying to confront her father like a wife or soothe him like a mother, and feeling drained in the process. What had become of her own strivings, toward art for example? Had she given up in order to mother her father?

Presented with questions like these, it took Roberta only a week to come up with a response. She felt she had to stay till the family was straightened out. Until then she would have to protect her mother and the children from her father, from his derogatory talk, from his tyranny and his emotional distance. ''You all,'' Roberta observed painfully but somewhat grandly, ''are hanging on me.''

In her initial shock at Roberta's onslaught—Roberta had usually reserved her onslaughts for father—her mother responded, ''You are being selfish. You know we need everybody here if the family is to function.'' But as the initial shock wore off, her mother could acknowledge that she had felt like dying when Roberta left home for art school.

Within a couple of weeks, Roberta's mother was beginning to talk about finding ways to cope with her husband. The family began to mobilize itself to face the real issue at hand: how they could give Roberta the freedom she had to have in order to become a productive person on her own terms, and how Roberta could begin to turn over to her mother and siblings their fair share of the stress from her father—in other words, how they could all get on with the family-life-cycle task of managing the first separation from the family.

Roberta's depression and confusion about art school could now be explored from a different perspective: as a crisis originating from the conflict between her strivings and the family's covert designation of what they wanted of her. Her freezing up when praised by a school staff member could be seen as one facet of her invisible loyalty to the family, the unconscious premise being, how can I enjoy contact with others when I have abandoned my family? Unless it was resolved, this unconscious bond to the family could interfere with Roberta's efforts to form both personal and working relationships. The therapeutic focus on what was happening on the productive side of Roberta's life was the point at which the grip of this covert family loyalty began to be recognized and challenged.

3

Designation

In the preceding chapter, we referred to the tensions that occur between the family and the growing child over the issues of
what the child is to do and how. In exploring career issues with
clients, whether or not they sought help for career problems, we
discovered that in a significant minority of cases, the struggle between child and family had gone so deep that its effect was to
set up an invisible obstacle in the way of career growth. Although
the number of clients presenting this pattern full-blown was
relatively small, we believe that what we found has broad implications for a larger population in which the pattern exerts a
significant influence even though it does not emerge quite so
vividly.

THE INVISIBLE OBSTACLE

With these clients one theme appeared to recur. The words
of this theme vary, but the idea remains constant: ''Something
is holding me back,'' ''I get to a certain point and then I can't
get beyond it,'' ''On a scale of one to ten I never get beyond
seven. Or as soon as I get to ten I slip back,'' ''It's as if a leash

jerked me back.'' These observations by different clients all convey a sense of severe frustration in the face of some invisible obstacle that continues to stand in their way.

FEAR OF ACHIEVEMENT

It is sufficient here to acknowledge, without providing a review of, the studies dealing with fear of achievement based on psychoanalytic principles that deal with fear of achievement. These include the talion principle, the child's fear that there will be retaliation if the child sets up a rivalry with the parent. In the myth of Icarus, who tried to fly higher than his father and crashed into the sea, it was not the father who engineered the fall; it was fate calling Icarus to account for his conceit. The notion that "pride goeth before a fall," that whomever the gods wish to strike down they first make proud, or fate is just waiting to take a whack at anybody who sticks his or her neck out too far, appears in most cultures. Avoidance of achievement can also be linked to such states as depression, masochism, the narcissistic fear of failure, and the fear of giving up a dependent relationship that is providing gratification to both its members.

DESIGNATION

The Invisible Parameters

But what we wish to address is a special relationship in which dynamics more powerful than those just mentioned may keep an individual bound by invisible yet seemingly unbreakable restraints. When we shift the focus from inner dynamics to family process, we see that out of the interaction between child and family a designation of the child's place in the family emerges. It is as if an object had been placed in orbit in a particular relationship to the objects around it. In the beginning, the designation has to do with how the child will make him- or herself useful to the family. It may be explicit but is more often covert.

Transient and Lasting Designations

In some respects the designation may be a transient one; for example, one child may be scapegoated until he or she leaves home, at which time the next sibling assumes the position of scapegoat; or a mother may compel her child to become a confidant until she finds a new lover. But in some cases the child's occupancy of a designated position appears to acquire permanence. What has by now become a classic designation, and one with which we will be very much concerned, is for the child to provide some function that is lacking in the relationship between the parents, and without which it appears that the well-being or even the survival of the family could not be preserved. An example would be that of the child who provides mother with emotional nurturance she cannot obtain from her husband. Another would be that of the child who, by using any of a wide variety of strategies, manages to deflect the parents' hostilities away from each other and toward the child instead. Another would be the child who assumes the burden of emotional support for a chronically depressed parent.

The Involvement of Siblings

A child's designation may also have to do with what is going on between a parent and another sibling. If the older brother is continually engaged in fights with the father that have a disruptive effect on the family, the younger brother may learn to stay in the background, keep quiet, and find indirect ways of bringing his own needs to his father's attention. This can have a profound effect later on on the way he handles his relationships with his employer and his wife. If the older brother earns the mantle of "troublemaker," the one who follows in his footsteps may be designated for life as the "good little boy."

Extrafamily Events

Lasting designations have to do with events outside the family as well as with intrafamily dynamics. One child may be picked out, for instance, as the one who is going to carry the banner of great accomplishment into the next generation. This burden can get heavier if the child is charged with the task of making it up to the family for a father who failed or for a sibling who died. The designation can go in any direction. The implication or injunction that "you will end right where you began" can be just as binding as "you will succeed for all of us." The designation may, of course, be multiple; e.g., a child may be expected simultaneously to give up any hope of personal achievement and remain home to be a bastion of emotional support for mother.

Contradictory Designations

The designation may be split, with each parent feeding in a message that contradicts the other's. This category would include the child whom the mother selects to carry forward her hopes of literary greatness. The father, meanwhile, might be trying to teach his child that what counts is what you can do with your hands. The mother's emphasis on things of the mind may take on an extra edge if she despises the father and his calluses. The child thus bound by a split designation could not get far in any direction without a crippling sense of disloyalty.

The contradictions may be exacerbated in cases in which one parent projects a bad part of his or her own self-image onto the child. This might be expressed on occasion through outbursts like, "I've never seen a child like you, you belong in a reform school." The other parent might then leap in to defend the child, shouting, "How can you say such horrible things?" Even if the latter parent's intention is simply to defend the child, the child becomes instantly and painfully aware that he or she is the focus of hostility between the parents. But it is also possible that one parent will seize the opportunity to come to the defense of the child in order to vent his or her own hostility toward the other. *Both* parents may be using the child as a means of externalizing their own inner conflicts.

The fact that each parent contradicts the other might make it appear that, far from having a designated place in the family, the child is simply being buffeted about. However, this may be one of the most compelling kinds of designations. The child cannot consciously identify what is being expected of him or her, yet the child's presence may enable both parents to act out their own conflicts in such a way that it does not destroy the marriage, because the focus is kept on the child instead of on the marital relationship. Thus the child's designated place becomes that of the stabilizer, often a difficult role to reconcile later in life with legitimate self-assertion.

The Messages of Designation

The messages of designation may be couched in various implicit or explicit terms. These may include:

"Don't do it."
"You must do it."
"Don't be visible."
"Don't be."
"Do it but don't identify with it, say instead that you were doing it for someone else."
"When you do that you are acting just like your father."
"Do it but be very careful, because something bad is bound to happen."
"You may do it but you must not enjoy it."
"Just because you are a female doesn't mean you can't do anything you want to do—but don't try it, you might get hurt."
"If it was such a good idea, somebody else would have already done it."

Of course these messages can have various extrafamilial sources, including religious and cultural values and superstitions. But whatever their original source, they may be brought to bear upon the child primarily because this serves the unique needs of this particular family to reinforce the messages of designation.

The Influence of Reality

Obviously the realities impinging on a child will also have effects on the child's designation. An oldest sibling is more likely to be charged with the burden of being caretaker to the younger siblings. The death of a parent can disrupt the designations of all the siblings. A change in the family's financial status may have a profoundly restrictive effect, or it may spur one or more of the children to greater effort, sometimes at the cost of throwing the rest of their lives out of balance.

FAMILY LEGACY

The Effects of Legacy

While the precise position the child occupies may be influenced by current realities such as a business failure by the father, which puts more pressure on the next generation for achievement, it may turn out that the child can shift position only within the limits set by a mandate that has come down from previous generations of the family. We are indebted to Boszormenyi-Nagy (Boszormenyi-Nagy & Ulrich, 1981) for calling attention to the importance of this phenomenon, to which he has applied the term *legacy*. We mentioned the younger brother who keeps a low profile so as not to add to the disruption his father and brother are causing within the family. This younger brother's movements may at the same time be circumscribed by a family legacy that dictates that the oldest son must be the achiever, while the younger son is to accentuate his older brother's status by remaining a dependent. It appears that legacy is often the most powerful determinant of the child's position in the family.

Legacy can either enable or restrict, as the above example suggests. Paradoxically, a legacy that mandates achievement can be oppressive, if it requires the child to devote a lifetime of effort to the fulfillment of the legacy. Sometimes the lines drawn by legacy seem clearly defined, as when it dictates that the child can never go beyond the point of success reached by the father. More often there is no such clearly defined restriction, and the influence of legacy is less explicit without being any less binding.

It is our impression that the invisible dictates of legacy can be as coercive as those of any primitive superego. Indeed, it seems likely that the dictates of legacy are reinforced by the demands of the superego. Multigenerational legacy also acquires an aura of survival value. People come to be venerated partly because their longevity is testimony to their ability to survive. Patterns that resulted in survival before are expected to ensure it again, so they may be pursued no matter what the cost. Shifting to new patterns means facing the unknown and courting disaster. One woman always cut her hams in two before baking them. When asked why, she reacted with surprise. That was the way her mother did it. When it was suggested that she research the matter, she came back to report that her mother had not been able to afford a larger baking pan.

Legacy: A Controversial Concept

We are aware that the concept of legacy may not be readily acceptable in America, which is supposed to be a place where people came to throw off their old bonds and roam at will. But that definition has itself become a legacy, one of the invisible effects of which may be for people to find it hard to acknowledge and deal with their rootedness. This cultural value is reflected, it seems, in some of the literature on personal development. In speaking of psychosocial factors, for instance, Erikson (1968) makes no clear-cut distinction between the effects of the family and of other components of society; likewise, Levinson (1978), in presenting his observations on men's career cycles, makes only passing reference to the matter of family legacy.

Ethnic factors may, of course, have a profound significance for legacy, an extreme instance being the caste system in which, for the upper castes, doing manual work is unthinkable. It may be equally unthinkable for a member of a low caste to leave his rural area and move into a town to live and work. Doing so may mean forfeiting any claim to a place in the family. Ethnic groups vary widely, of course, in their emphasis on the child's putting his or her resources back into the family.

Indigenous Legacies

In many cases, however, the legacy appears to have been created within the family. For example, the legacy may dictate that the women of successive generations will do almost all of their giving to their fathers and sons and very little to their husbands. The legacy may take the form of a specific injunction: The son is to become an M.D. because his father did or is to become an M.D. because his father did not so he "must make it" for the whole family. This can put the child in a bind, unable or unwilling to fulfill the family expectation yet unable to move out to a position from which an independent decision could be made. Or the child's legacy may be to take on the burden of living out the interrupted life of an older sibling who has died. In one family, soon after the oldest son's death, the next oldest formally requested that he be allowed to take his brother's name.

In contrast to legacies of high expectation, an individual's legacy may dictate that he or she prepare for a lifetime of ducking under low bridges. One bright and perceptive client told how her parents' lives had been tightly circumscribed by learning disabilities; she then observed,

> It's as if I signed a pact on my birthday that I would stay with them in this. I had to be part of the pact. The three of us would be OK together, not like other people. . . . Three years ago I was attempting to ask my mother if I could break the contract. I tried to talk but she wouldn't allow it. I felt really bad, as if I were doing a mean thing.

Permission Slips

The legacy may be that the child can accomplish only what he or she has been directed by someone else to accomplish. In one family, the wife carried the whole burden of raising the children, taking care of the house and yard, making all of the arrangements for the overseas moves required by her husband's work, etc.

Throughout the years of their marriage, his principal contribution other than money was to tell his wife to do each of the things she did—to get the house painted, buy a new car, order the airline tickets, etc. Finally his boredom with this one-sided way of life became so extreme that he threatened to leave.

This precipitated a panic in her. Without what she regarded as his "permission slips," she held the unwavering conviction that she would be totally immobilized, unable to work, unable to care for herself, the house, or the remaining child.

Her reliance on this granting of permission by someone other than herself appeared to have its roots in her childhood in Norway. Her father had called on her for heroic efforts in school and sports without ever acknowledging that her successes stemmed from any intrinsic worth within herself. Her taking part in the underground resistance to Germany at direct risk to her own life was considered simply a matter of doing what she was told. The father's attitude may have been in accordance with cultural patterns, and the intensity of his treatment of her may have suggested something about his own emotional involvement; yet it would still be important to explore whether his withholding of any acknowledgment was consistent with the way men had treated their wives and daughters in this family.

In another, similar situation, a woman who was first in line to become comptroller of a corporation actually sat in silence while her husband complacently described how he had taught her how to use a checkbook. Without his OK, she said later, she found it hard to act. "It just seemed like I had to get everybody's approval. I couldn't do anything unless it was *right.*" Concerning whatever she had achieved, this woman lived as if the ledger of her accomplishments was revised to zero every night and she had to start out from scratch the next morning to validate her claim to competence.

The Withholding of Support

It is equally possible, of course, for the male to receive messages that will inhibit his functioning. An embittered father, unable to accept the restrictions that had been placed upon his own life, reproached his young son at the dinner table with, "You got the best steak." The size of the steak became a precise measure of where the son was supposed to stand in relation to the parent. When the son eventually became a vice-president, the father was standing by, shaking his head. "This means you have farther to fall." When the son bought a colonial house in the suburbs the father's message was simply, "You can't afford it." Such a parental attitude runs counter to our assumption that parents live for the success of their children, but the demonstrable fact is that there are parents from all walks of life who, for reasons often linked to family legacy, are unable to give their children acknowledgment or a message of support, and this has a profound effect upon the child's position in the family. Legacy therefore can be seen to play a profound part in the shaping of designated positions.

THE PARENTS' INVESTMENT IN DESIGNATION

We are employing the term *designation* to refer to the way the family makes use of the child. We do not mean to suggest, of course, that it is unusual to expect a child to be useful to the family. This occurs naturally through the child's very presence. It ordinarily includes the child's gradually taking over the duties of self-care, doing family chores, observing family routines, and providing a link to the neighbors. The child will be deprived if he or she does not have to face age-appropriate responsibilities. The critical question is whether the parents intend to prepare the child to accept responsibilities on a larger scale outside the family, or whether the intent is to bind the child to produce for the family at the expense of his or her legitimate interests elsewhere.

Documentation From the Literature

The fact that parents' needs lead them to use children in various exploitative ways has, of course, been well documented in the literature on the family. We shall cite only a few examples. Sperry, Staver, Reiner, and Ulrich (1954) described a family pattern in which the younger sibling was expected to renounce claims to self-assertion on behalf of a more successful, preferred sibling, the result being a severe functional learning disability.

Boszormenyi-Nagy and Spark (1973) spoke of the "parentification" of the child, an example being the preadolescent child who moves back and forth as a pendulum, alternately reassuring each parent as he or she stresses his or her own incompetence. The parents' threats of divorce can be a means to halt the emancipation of the burdened child. Boszormenyi-Nagy and Spark also described, among various syndromes, that of the "well sibling" who conceals feelings of emptiness and depletion to keep up a facade of health, while providing "reason and organization to the entire chaotic family." Such a child may eventually find it impossible to shift attention from home to college.

Stierlin et al. (1980) referred to delegation and binding. The child may be delegated to carry out a mission, not necessarily a pathological one; but the delegation can be "derailed" if the child lacks the needed ability, if it conflicts with another delegation, or if it requires the child to be disloyal to the other parent. In addition, the child may be "bound," i.e., imprisoned in various ways by the needs of the parents. To us it seems curious that Stierlin did not mention the child's own preferences as a factor that could conflict with the delegated mission.

Slipp (1984) related the way the child is made use of to the pathology of the parent or parents. A borderline parent, for instance, may project a good-parent image on the child, who is then expected to think and act in such a way as to preserve the marriage or even preserve the cohesion of the projecting parent.

THE CHILD'S INVESTMENT IN THE DESIGNATION

Loyalty

The study of family process has led also to greater appreciation of the part the child plays in maintaining his or her own position in the family. It can sometimes be seen that the child is making an enormous investment in his or her designated position, both in defining and preserving it. For instance, the younger brother who maintains a very low profile, acts as peacemaker between his older brother and father, and learns how merely to hint at his own needs may well be developing a kind of talent. Even if it is at his own expense, his whole life may pivot around this peacemaker theme. Boszormenyi-Nagy and Spark (1973) have called attention to the child's family loyalty as a central motivating factor. The very fact of being born into the family provides the starting point for the child's loyalty. It is reinforced by whatever the family does on the child's behalf, but we find that the depth of the child's loyalty cannot be gauged simply by the extent of the benefits received. Loyalty provides fuel for adherence to the terms of the family legacy, whether or not this is actually beneficial to the child.

It is not surprising that loyalty received relatively little attention in psychologies that focused upon intrapsychic events. The significance of loyalty is its presence in a reciprocal relationship. A deep synergism of values and interests exists between the child and the family into which it is born. This force intensifies loyalty even in the absence of parental good deeds. By the time the child is old enough to sense where he or she belongs in the family, loyalty is operating to hold the child in place.

Even though it receives little attention in the psychoanalytic literature, we are quite familiar in daily life with the power of the child's loyalty. In a situation where an upwardly mobile young father was putting extreme pressure for achievement on his six-year-old son, the therapist sought to open explorations of the child's feelings by eliciting an expression of loyalty to the father; this might relieve the child's discomfort about discussing family affairs with a stranger. The therapist asked, "On a scale of one to ten, how would you rate your father?" The son promptly replied, "Fifteen." The father, embarrassed because his son did not seem to have grasped the question, intervened: "The doctor said the top number was ten." To this the child replied just as promptly, "Other daddies are ten."

Approaching similar phenomena from an object-relations perspective, Wetzel (1984) observes that for the individual suffering introjective depression, to be separate and to succeed is to be disloyal to the object of one's love. Here the loyalty is seen as operating between the child and the object, rather than between the child and the family. This notion that the child can be bound into a no-win situation by the strength of its loyalty is common to both the object relations and the systemic approaches.

Terror

Other factors besides loyalty may be operating, of course, to hold the child in the designated position. In a disturbed family, one of these may be terror. The child may feel that the alternative to losing the designated place in the family is to have no place at all. In one situation where a therapist was helping an adult client to work through a traumatic loss, the therapist arrived at the observation that the client was experiencing the same sense of abandonment and terror that a little girl might feel. The client replied that she had never felt terror as a little girl because she had been able to function well enough to ward off abandonment, whereas her brother had not. The therapist might have said that the client was now experiencing the terror she had succeeded in staving off as a child through her own energetic realization of her place in the family.

Seen in this context, "maternal rejection" may be not only an emotional turnoff but a threatened or actual ejection of the child from his or her accustomed place. Later in life, to step outside of the place dictated by legacy may be a self-imposed rejection, equivalent to cutting off one's roots and stepping into a void. Besides the violation of invisible loyalty, such an act may generate intolerable feelings of fear, guilt, and depression.

Grandiosity

It is also our impression that childish grandiosity may play into the child's efforts to maintain position. Often, as we have already observed, the child perceives his or her position to be that of peacemaker for older members of the family. Especially when these include the parents, the child may feel the burden of keeping the family intact. To varying degrees, other family members may indeed regard the child as the redeemer, not for some future time but now.

Infantile grandiosity may thus get a considerable boost from reality, and the child's sense of having to take care of the family may acquire an intense, even desperate quality. One client, speaking of the acute conflicts between his mother and father, observed that, "Somebody could have saved the day by doing the right thing at the right time, and I was a candidate." Another said of his mother's alcoholism,

> Since I was a little kid I have been irritated at my mother about her drinking. She was a mean, rotten drunk, one of the worst. She would pick fights, spew venom. I watched it, I said, "Do something about it," but she wouldn't, and I don't forgive her. When you've put so much into it, trying to get her to stop—I tried everything over the years. I tried every trick. I became her enemy.

Asked if this was a great disappointment, the client replied, "The disappointment was in yourself because you were not strong enough (to make her stop)."

Attempting to sort out why he felt like "nothing" in spite of a successful professional career, one client included among the top three reasons the fact that he had not been able to save his mother, who had been permanently hospitalized with a psychosis when he was eight years old.

> I couldn't bring her to normal, I couldn't wish her or pray her well or create a situation where I could save my mother. And it's so frustrating, because I know that as a kid I wanted to save my mother. I didn't hate her in the beginning, I just finally became so frustrated, and that's something I've just recently surfaced. I know I felt an enormous amount of frustration that my mother wouldn't get well. I knew that I was far cleverer than an ordinary small child. I knew this about myself, so I took the responsibility on myself in some way of trying to help.

And then finally I tossed in the towel. I said, "Forget it," and then I got to hate her, because she was a source not only of misery in that house but of my own failure.

We believe that if a statement like this about the concerns of a child sounds strange to adult ears, it is because as adults we have lost touch with some of the painful preoccupations of children, and developmental studies that take children out of their family context do not recapture how concerned children can be about those relationships.

The obsessive and often obnoxious efforts of the adult to control events may echo the child's early, apprehensive sense of being the only one around who can look after things properly, e.g., "But, Daddy, what if we have *two* flat tires?" (See the case of Peter, p. 40.)

The Significance of the Family of Origin

There are many ways to characterize the importance to the child of his or her place in the family. In narcissistic terms, there may be a basic hunger for admiration, for "somebody to show it to" when you have just won your first track trophy. In object-relations terms, the goal may be to preserve or restore the connection to the significant object or to preserve the significant object when its existence is threatened. In family-process terms, the child may be trying to maintain a family enmeshment that yields a sense of unity and wards off the fear of loss.

For our purposes, the significant thing about all these motivations, including loyalty, is that they are addressed to maintaining a place in the *family of origin*; they all have to do with the child's usefulness *within* the family. Depending upon the nature of legacy and other factors, these motivations may take priority over and impede the cultivation of the child's independent strivings.

From our observations it appears that efforts exerted on behalf of the family may easily come to feel "real," whereas efforts targeted outside the parameters of one's designated place in the

family may not seem real because the family has no investment
in them. One family may make the boundaries loose enough to
embrace achievement at school or at work. In another family, the
only effort that counts may be the child's effort to provide direct
emotional support for a depressed father or mother. For the child,
then, this may be the only effort that feels "real." A therapist
of our acquaintance was never permitted within her family of
origin to identify any act of hers as an achievement. When she
had completed her training and her private caseload began filling up, she found herself waking up in the morning not feeling
like her "real self" anymore. Instead, she felt "incongruent."
A client expressed what we believe to be a similar attitude about
buying a new car, a top-of-the-line model. "It was OK to have
a Beetle, but this is for *grown-ups*. I feel—I'm going to pay the
price. I have no right to this. I'll pay."

Another client had described how when he was a small boy
it troubled him to see his mother getting exhausted while he sat
in a corner of the restaurant waiting until she finished waiting
on tables and could take him home. His mother had expressed
the wish, "Maybe someday you'll be good and take care of
everything." Instead, after trying various kinds of jobs, he found
himself working as a waiter. "So I failed her too. I'm now in her
exact position and I can't break out of it or move ahead." Yet,
speaking of his attempts to move into a different kind of work,
he observed, "I don't feel like I'm attaching myself to something
that's me."

Of course in each of the above instances the process of individuation is incomplete. We are suggesting that this is because
the person's sense of realness is tied to the early struggle to perform the acts of value that were designated by the family of
origin. If there was no encouragement when the child achieved
something outside the family, like winning a track trophy, the
child could feel, "What's the use, there's nobody to show it to."
We have heard a grown-up, who was about to sell for a very
substantial profit a company he had developed, express the same
feeling: "There's nobody to show it to." Speaking of how she
had done the same work as the men in a bank and had fought

for raises for fifteen years until she was earning a good salary, one client commented, "I never took it seriously." We believe that she must have taken it very seriously and then covered this over with denial so her family would not perceive her as an ambitious person. She had never been able to share her successes with her family.

The Sense of Futility

Even if the achievement of the adult does not violate the mandate he or she received as a child or if the success of the adult is as originally prescribed by the parents, the success may still seem unreal because the parents' acknowledgment may not take the form the child always dreamed of. The parent who seemed depressed and empty-handed before may still seem so now. The parent who was genuinely unable to express esteem for the child may still be unable to do so. The parents who, in the child's fantasy, would stop their drinking or their bickering with each other once certain gifts had been laid at their doorstep, may seem indifferent to those gifts once they are actually received. Perhaps by now they are too tired to notice. The long-yearned-for connection with the significant object has not been achieved after all. One woman described how she had encouraged visits from her siblings in the hope that they would take back to her father, who refused to come see her himself, some word of how well she had progressed in life. It did not work because her siblings were as intimidated by her successes as her father would have been. She commented, "I'm sad I couldn't have figured out a way to connect with him. As an adult, I couldn't come up with a way to make him understand." We believe it is this sense of futility that leads many people who have been accorded a high level of recognition by the outside world to feel that they are only "fakes," waiting for someone to catch them.

This seeking of a sense of confirmation can permeate one's efforts at achievement and cause discouragement with the results. The woman with a good position in corporate finance who allowed her husband to show her how to use a checkbook was, as she explained it, unable to function without approval. As a child, she had taken the place of a father who refused to become involved, and sat up at night with her mother who seemed to be having attacks of angina. The daughter believed that if left alone the mother would die. But she was unable to relieve her mother's suffering from the physical pain, father's indifference, or things in her mother's own childhood that still made her suffer. Thus the daughter felt she had never done enough, and she lived in dread that if she did not do more the family would collapse around her, and found herself unable to have any intrinsic faith in her own capacities. This remained true in spite of her distinct and significant achievements.

The Effects on Achievement

The child's perception of how he or she is to serve the family may thus be at odds with the emergence of individual strivings based on an inner sense of one's own interests and capacities, as stimulated by peers and teachers as well as by members of the family. In our experience, the tug-of-war between the family's and the child's preferences may have a profound effect upon that child's eventual choice of what to do as well as on how effectively this choice will be carried out.

THE FORCE OF DESIGNATION

The cases of Peter and Edith illustrate the subtle but powerful force of designation. Peter was bound by a mandate to achieve; Edith was bound by the prohibition of achievement. Peter experienced distress; Edith experienced despair.

Peter

Whenever Peter and his family went for a drive, Peter would revive a question that his father could not put to rest: "But, Daddy, what if we have *two* flat tires?" Peter was then eight. At 38 he was a millionaire, about whom his mother remarked: "He is always so tense that I am dreadfully worried for his health.'' His wife had gone past the point of being worried; she had started giving ultimatums that things must change if she were to stay; and in his efforts to change he had managed only to compound the conflict.

Peter's great-grandfather, a blacksmith, had been decorated posthumously during the War of 1870 for loading his wagon with scrap iron and employing it to sideswipe an advancing column of German troops. This act showed a clear regard for *La Gloire et La Patrie*. Peter's grandpapa, born shortly before the event, grew up in the ambience of having a very special, even if absent, father. He married the daughter of a prominent family and was soon so affronted by his in-laws' shutting their doors on him that he took his bride to America, vowing that here he would make a fitting place for himself and his family. By combining a flair for design and marketing, and a sense of the family's destiny, he made a successful entry into the growing market for electric light fixtures for New York's more elegant houses and offices.

The business flourished so well that Peter's father, as a young man, was able to give himself over to airplanes and imported automobiles, for which he developed a passion. But with the collapse of the economy in 1929, his father gave up his cars and planes and stepped in to rescue the family business. It could be saved, he realized, only by laying off much of the shop crew and cutting the pay of the remainder. To this task he devoted his natural pervasive charm, tempered by a toughness obtained through countless hours in the company of airplane and auto mechanics.

Perceiving that his son's career was moving into its ascendancy and that the family had indeed been rescued, Peter's grandpapa withdrew grumpily into his flower garden, while Peter's father proceeded to rebuild the company. During this period, Peter's mother, in the tradition of the Wellesley girls of her time, took lessons from Grandmama in the self-effacing advancement of her husband's interests. When Peter arrived, Grandmama made certain that his mother set out at once to groom him for his future role in the family. When Peter toddled into a room, no matter who was present, his mother soon diverted the conversation to focus on her son. Before he had fully relinquished the bottle, Peter had begun to be aware that the mantle of preserving the family fortunes would one day be on his shoulders.

By the age of eight, he was beginning to tender hints, as in his question about the second flat tire, that he was not wholly satisfied by his father's management of things. Later his doubts were to be confirmed by reality, for his father, mistaking the easy response he got from people for an endorsement of his company's products, vastly overestimated his market share and drove the company into bankruptcy.

By then Peter was ready. At his family's urgings he had attended engineering school, decided that it was time for new directions, and shrewdly estimated that there would be a demand in the emerging high-technology industries for a particular array of switching devices available only in Germany. He soon became sole importer for the equipment, drew on his engineering skills to adapt the imported equipment to the complex needs of his customers, made himself indispensable to them, and was soon drawing commissions that would have turned Grandmama's family green with envy.

Like his father, he soon had five foreign cars in his garage. But unlike him, he scarcely had time to drive them, let alone tinker or polish. He had found suitable living arrangements for his mother and father, to whom he paid flying visits between his flights to Germany, his customers scattered about the U.S., his son by a quickly expired first marriage, now in boarding school, and, finally, to his home, where his new wife was barely able to keep on top of everything that piled up in his absence.

There could not be the slightest question in anyone's mind that Peter had fulfilled the part in life designated by his family, but now nobody knew how to get him to stop. He made impromptu efforts at relaxing, like dashing into the garage for an hour with a polishing cloth or by making more elaborate efforts involving weekends in the Bahamas. But these served only to add to the tension, both for him and his wife, who was bothered enough already by the fact that three of the cars would not run and the swimming pool was filling up with debris. When her objections began to sound terminal, Peter did manage to find time to undertake marital therapy with her.

Initial explorations soon led in the direction of his legacy, and after nearly a year of intermittent work on the legacy and its impact, Peter was showing a very marked "mellowing." He was not sure why, but now enough time and energy were becoming available to look at other aspects of his life and marriage that deserved attention. It had become evident that the designation that drove Peter to go so far in his career had left out any preparation for a balancing of his career with the other vital aspects of living.

Edith

Edith's father helped her with her homework until her younger brother Matthew began first grade. Then when John reached first first grade, he helped Matthew and John. When Jean reached first grade, he continued to help Matthew and John.

Her father worked in a cannery, but he was a man of enough intelligence to remember the Latin he had learned in a one-room schoolhouse. Edith's mother was 17 when she married Edith's father. He brought Edith up like the other children, which included giving her beatings until the boys were old enough to make him stop. Her mother augmented her father's wages by raising vegetables for cash, so the family lived better than most in their valley. When her mother questioned her father's approach to things, his response was quite explicit: "Who gave you the right to think?"

Edith worked hard in school and read every book she could find. "I was killing myself inside," she said. "I yearned to have him notice me." He encouraged the boys, but with the constant reminder that the world outside the valley was an unsafe place and that they should find their lives somewhere on this side of the mountains.

Her father did not find it easy, however, to make a place for Edith in his view of the valley. If she had only stayed in her mother's shadow like Jean, he would have spared Edith any response at all. When she tried to argue with him, his response was, "Who gave *you* the right to think?" When one of the boys tried to tell him that Edith had done something well, his response was simply, "She's got you hoodwinked." When she drove the tractor, he waited until she made a mistake and then told her to stay off it. When she brought the car home through a snowstorm, he shouted at her for not staying off the roads. When she got married at nineteen, he said she was too young and he didn't go to the wedding.

During the next twenty years, Edith struggled to put herself through college, worked, outgrew her husband, remarried, worked again. She became hugely successful at organizing and teaching aerobics classes. She found she could do anything she set out to do as long as she could deny the importance of both her effort and her achievement. She was just an amateur, she would say. Or her husband had given her the OK. Or it was her students through whom she was expressing herself. "My students *are* me," she said. Edith quite genuinely believed she had the world "hoodwinked," as if she were somehow leading people to believe she was highly competent while concealing the "real self" that was ready to burst with fear and self-doubt. When her therapist suggested that the person wholly lacking in self-confidence was not the real self either, Edith replied, "Behind that door lies darkness." What this meant, we believe, is captured in a quote from Wetzel (1984): "It is not the personhood of many women that needs to be changed, but their self-perception. They are already self-reliant and they do not recognize themselves" (p. 103).

Achievement never did anything to dispel Edith's self-doubt. While speaking of one of her accomplishments, the management of a church bazaar that brought in record-making proceeds, she told her therapist,

> From somewhere, feelings came to stop me. As if something was saying, "It wasn't you." Almost like, if I accepted credit for it, something bad would happen. *Bad*, I mean that I would have an accident, or be sick.

And on the occasion of another success:

> It seemed as if I was able to understand, to feel as if I knew
> what a person needed, or what a situation needed, and do it,
> but yet it seemed as if something or someone was always there
> with a great big board, knocking me back, not accepting it.

When Edith did something that openly required her to take
the initiative on her own behalf, such as purchasing an auto-
mobile or a house, she would experience a pain that was so intense that there was nothing she could do about it. Crying did
not help. The only thing that relieved it was going to bed and
going to sleep. After the purchase of the car, she felt this way
for a day. After buying the house, she was in bed asleep for three
days before she recovered. She described other somatic symptoms that seemed to occur at times of overt achievement, such
as shaking uncontrollably or abruptly finding herself unable to
count out money from her purse. These were the kinds of bar-
riers she struggled to overcome while working, raising a daughter, and nursing her second husband through a severe illness.
The severity of the symptoms seemed to provide an accurate
gauge of how far she had stepped outside of the cramped space
designated for her during childhood.

One episode served to bring her conflict into perhaps a sharper
awareness than anyone should have to endure. At the worst
stage of her husband's illness, which occurred when they were
in France for his work, Edith received an urgent plea from her
father to come home.

> I can still see the whole scene. It had already been a stressful
> two days when I got home . . . Daddy was sitting in his chair.
> Literally, even the minute I walked in, it was, "Come and sit
> down by me." And then he just started talking, and talking,
> and talking.

The subject was his will, his concern that one brother might resent it if the other performed all the functions of executor, or even
that the job would be too big for either brother to handle alone.

It was just nonstop, I can still see his eyes . . . they were desperate, he was begging for me to help him . . . And I just sat there, and I thought, "If he doesn't shut up," and I just felt like breaking something . . . like really destroying something, to make it stop. But I felt that way with him. And I left.

There was something else, too, that while he was talking, for just a minute, I could see—it was as if I was up here watching the whole thing—I could see, our family and our little group, and Daddy had never ever been further than three towns away, except when he was in the war, because this was his security, and my brothers and sister were right there, and it was as if nobody could get away, because if they got away they couldn't function. And I had to get away. I had to, it was stronger than me, and I'm sorry, I'm sorry about so many things, but I couldn't—I just couldn't stay . . . like, it was strangling me, it was killing me.

And Daddy said, "Edith, please don't leave, if you leave the boys will blame me, they'll say I drove you away, if you leave I'll have a heart attack." I think I said to him, "If I stay here I'm going to absolutely go mad." And I kissed him goodbye. He pushed me away. I didn't hate him, you understand.

Thus with violent feelings Edith tried again to throw off the yoke of the family. That her father would ask her to give up her own life and come home to be her brothers' helper was an unbearably familiar event. But the desperation and pleading in her father's eyes went beyond this event. For a moment, Edith and her father were both looking at something he had no way to acknowledge. He could see that as things had turned out the family might not make it without her, but to open up this vista, to give it the reality of putting it in words would be to collapse the whole system on which the family was built. Edith had said, "Behind that door lies darkness," and this was what lay behind the door. In one respect her father and Edith were equal: Both were helpless victims of their own parts in the system of the family as each had learned it. When her father's desperation brought him so close to a breakthrough, Edith could only slam the door.

The urgent departure from her father's house could do nothing to free Edith from her captive part in the family. Even if we did not already know this, it is evident enough from the nature of the symptoms she reported when she began treatment. What realistic steps one can take, with or without therapeutic help, to rewrite the terms of one's designation will be the subject of a later chapter.

4

Carrying Patterns From
Home to Work

No one walking into the cool, gray, impersonal lobby of a Fortune 500 corporation headquarters would get the impression that this was a family affair. After some consideration, one might begin to wonder if the massive gray interior, untouched by anything but professionally selected plants and objects of art, had been erected as a barricade to keep the turbulent tide of human passions, including family process, from flooding the building and engulfing its occupants.

The lobby of the building bespeaks a rational structure of enormous power and solidity. But it is obvious that whatever is going on inside is being conducted by people; in order to function, they require systems, and the systems active inside the building have evolved out of, and continue to interact with, the systems outside, of which the family system is the most meaningful. It is not suprising if the corporate designers have sought, in the architecture and organization charts, to construct an environment that will transcend the systemic pushes and pulls. But this is just shoveling against the tide. Family systems influence and interact with organization structure, in both subtle and blatant ways, if for no other reason than the fact that the organization is made up of individuals who move between one set of systemic influences and the other.

THE CARRY-OVER OF DESIGNATED PATTERNS

We have suggested that individual growth is marked by tensions between the kinds of usefulness designated for a person by the family and the person's own productive strivings. As the person enters the workplace, there is no magical changeover to a new and clearly defined pattern of functioning. On the contrary, the previous tensions may be accentuated. This is partly because the new situation is full of ambiguity. Neither the interpersonal systems at work nor the instrumental aspects of the job itself may get clarified for a long time. The heightening of tension will also be due to what is happening inside the person, for there is now a multiple tug-of-war going on. There is the self designated by the family, which may be felt as "real," there is the would-be self, and now there is the self-of-expedience that one must cultivate just to survive in the new environment, and that may or may not align itself with either of the others.

Of course the pattern carried from home to work is not often so maladaptive as to lead to serious disruption of an individual's working life. But as with many other kinds of disturbances, the study of individuals who have encountered real trouble throws light on a process that can be considered universal.

As the new worker gets started, the predominant feeling may be, "What if they catch on?" In other words, what if they catch a glimpse of the sensed "real self" inside with all its frailties? One client who was making rapid career strides described how he would go to the men's room several times a day to look in the mirror, comb his hair, and "make sure I'm still there."

Another told of his first months as a very junior member of a business organization that he had joined because it was "now or never" to secure a job. As he talked to other employees, he felt sometimes as if he were a tiny person located somewhere inside himself exerting a great effort to pull the puppet strings that made his outside work. His record showed that he was fully qualified for his present position, but if his previous track record in life were itself a flimflam, a series of successful efforts to pretend that he was not baby-brother-committed-to-staying-home, then he was just digging himself deeper and deeper into deception.

This discomfort was usually associated with a nagging feeling that he really belonged somewhere else, as if he had forgotten a terribly important obligation. An experience he had during World War II clearly revealed the origin of the feeling. As a junior officer on board an aircraft carrier, it had been his job to see that the airplanes were loaded with ammunition, bombs, rockets, etc. in time for every mission. During the three days preceding the assault on Iwo Jima, airplanes from his ship and others, along with cruisers and destroyers, had mounted a barrage against the island that built up to a crescendo at the zero hour when the landing craft surged toward the beach. During this period the Japanese had kept the U.S. fleet under kamikaze attack night and day. As the U.S. landing craft were heading for the beach, a mail boat pulled alongside our friend's carrier, and among the mail it delivered was a letter for him which began, "You should be home looking after the family business."

Whether it is the U.S. Navy, a Fortune 500 corporation, or any other workplace, some ghostly porter brings the baggage of family business in through the door. At first it was surprising to us to discover the extent to which family patterns are carried over into work. What came as even more of a surprise was the extent to which it seems possible for the individual to find, at work, actors who will lend themselves to the other parts needed to recreate the family drama. In the pursuit of data from groups and individual clients during the past five years, we have repeatedly observed the almost uncanny resemblance of these work patterns to early familial patterns. The dovetailing of the actors' parts at work sometimes seems to be as neat as the dovetailing of disturbed dynamics in marital couples. Invisible loyalties, for instance, can operate to keep the person locked into a stagnant work situation. To vindicate an incompetent parent, the person may stay locked into an ambivalent relationship with an incompetent supervisor. Moves from one job to another may be simply the last resort for getting out of a stuck position in a triangle.

THE QUESTION OF TRANSFERENCE

In addressing this phenomenon we are, of course, entering the territory of "transference," which has already been well mapped by psychoanalysts and others. The distinction here is that we are not talking simply of a one-to-one transference phenomenon, such as the transference a junior worker brings to a senior. We are referring to patterns that are best understood when three or more persons are involved. In the case of Mark in Chapter 1, it soon became evident that Mark was not simply in conflict with one or the other parent; it was the way he became involved in the relationship between his parents that created career problems for him. Likewise with The Dropout in Chapter 2: it was not just the relationship with a domineering father that created difficulties; it was the subjectively perceived need to defend the mother and the younger children from the father that kept The Dropout locked tightly into the family system. In Chapter 4, we will present a series of cases describing the carry-over of patterns from home to work; in all of these cases, the central feature is the fact that the person brings to work "family baggage," consisting of a pattern of relating to two or more other people.

It seems reasonable to assume that when a critical encounter, consisting of one event or a series of events, occurs at work between a junior person and a senior, transference and counter-transference reactions are quite likely to be triggered. It also seems reasonable to assume that when this triggering of transference occurs, it will tend to set off something else within the individual, that is, a regressive reactivation of being within the family-of-origin system. The individual to whom this is happening will then, for example, behave toward peers at work more like he or she behaved toward siblings, and toward a second senior perhaps as he or she behaved toward the other parent. Evidence of such responses occurs in some of our case material. From a logical point of view, it is hard to see why this would *not* happen.

If such a regressive reactivation of family-of-origin patterns occurs, it can be assumed that the individual will begin to apply
at work the same kinds of defective data processing that took
place to preserve the family system, i.e., avoidance, denial, projection, displacement, etc.

Designated by Default

Jill, 25, came to therapy to work on "personal" issues, meaning conflicts with her boyfriend and feelings of estrangement
from her parents. But it soon became clear that personal and work
issues were indistinguishable. Jill held a skilled position requiring the application of computer technology to operating problems
in a large corporation. But she had become discouraged and
frustrated because she believed she was getting only the most
routine assignments, that her position had no future in it, that
no one had any awareness of what she was capable of doing, and
that notices of openings elsewhere in the corporation were not
being routed to her. She felt like an outsider at work and seemed
to have no hope of getting in. She lived in fear of making stupid
mistakes that would confirm what she thought was the low opinion of her held by others.

Explorations in therapy disclosed that the most troubled period
of her life was when the family moved from Boston to New Lon-
don. Until that time she had been a straight A student, but in
the new school her capabilities were overlooked and she received
a D in science because she could not catch up with unfamiliar
materials. This horrified her, and her distress was heightened
by the fact that her parents seemed to be ignoring her school
problems. She felt overwhelmingly isolated and spent long hours
in her room alone.

Further exploration gradually brought to light that Jill's parents
tended to preserve rigid boundaries around their relationship,
from which all three of the children felt excluded. Her mother
and father were "best friends." Their daughter's efforts to be
helpful within the family, for instance by acting cheerful around

her father, were not acknowledged, and her isolation deepened.

This could be characterized as designation by default. That is, Jill could be most useful to the family if she held back, made herself invisible, and kept from exerting any stress. This was an instance of "less is more." Of course in reality the presence of the children in a semi-excluded state may have done much to reinforce the parents' sense of solidarity with each other. However, Jill had the nagging suspicion that to be nothing at all might serve best of all.

As we pursued this family pattern, Jill was encouraged to identify the positive contributions she had made, such as her persistent cheerfulness. She was also encouraged to open conversations with the parents about past events, although she was of course afraid she would distress them by doing so. Concurrently, she began talking to her siblings about the family and was amazed to learn how much their experiences within the family had paralleled hers. From feeling isolated, she moved toward being part of a sibling group.

As these changes occurred, a shift of perception about work began to take place. She opened up conversations with her supervisor and reported that the supervisor was not in fact distant and withholding. On the contrary, it turned out that she had become confident enough in Jill's ability to let Jill work on her own. "She knows I'll flag her if I need help." The routine nature of the job was dictated by external factors. And some of the people in the departments that made use of her services, Jill discovered, were impressed by her work; what was more, they were "fun to fool around with." This discovery came at first as a real "super-surprise." Jill could hardly believe that people would notice and remember her. Next, word began circulating about possible reorganizations and new opportunities. The tight clamp of the early family patterns on Jill was gradually being loosened.

We can speculate that Jill responded quickly because her parents had had no great investment in her "designation by default." She was allowed to be isolated; she was at the same time relatively free to break away from her isolation in whatever new direction she chose.

Don't Be Like Aunt Mildred

Like Jill, Susan had the job of introducing computer work into a department that was unfamiliar with it. Also like Jill, Susan's
initial concern was with her peers, particularly the secretaries at
the adjoining desks. In this case, it was a matter of not "know-
ing how to talk to them," but Susan was not suffering from any
social deficit; she meant that she did not know how to preserve
her poise when they took advantage of her, for instance, by leaving her to cover their telephones while she was engrossed in computer programming. "They just don't understand the intensity
of my work and when I try to explain they don't get the concept.
If I don't play with kid gloves on, they get upset." The supervisor of the department, it seemed, was too flustered to bring
any order into the situation.

It was not surprising to learn that Susan was the oldest of three
sisters. Her mother had been sick a lot, and Susan often stepped
in to take charge. Trying to monitor her siblings was heavy going; they claimed she was bossy and they did not want to listen
to her. When her mother regained her health enough to climb
back into the saddle, she gave Susan no gratitude. Obviously
it was clear to Susan's sisters that her authority was transient.
Years later, when Susan entered therapy, her sister Kathy
was still taking her clothes and Susan was still at a loss for
words.

Susan knew her mother had suffered severely in childhood
from a live-in aunt who had such a vicious tongue that she was
finally shunned by the family. As Susan was growing up, anyone
who sounded like Aunt Mildred got an instant rebuke. Her sisters
were able to put Susan down with devastating effect simply by
saying, "There you go, sounding just like Aunt Mildred again."
No one ever told Susan that she did *not* sound like Aunt Mildred.
Her father was pleasant and uninvolved; it would not have occurred to him to give Susan this kind of reassurance. As Susan's
story unfolded, it became clear that the resurgence at work of
her uncertainties about her place in her family had led to a crisis
of self-confidence.

Doomsday Panic

Ted, a 42-year-old lawyer, came into treatment because he was experiencing a nearly immobilizing anxiety attack that he labeled his "doomsday panic." These panic attacks had occurred throughout Ted's adult life. This one had been triggered when he had been asked to testify in a case involving a dispute between two advertising agencies over the terms of a contract Ted had helped prepare. One litigant had subpoenaed Ted with the expectation that his testimony would be conclusive. Ted's panic centered around the conviction that once the suit was underway, both litigants would join in attacking him as culpable because of negligence in the phrasing of the contract terms. Ted was obsessed by fear of losing his present job, his home, and all his property. "I know I'll be out selling syrup on Route 7."

Ted, an only child, believed his panic related to how he had been parented. His father disciplined him not only by shunning him for periods of up to a month but also by making explicit threats. "I love you, but if you do this again I'll really cut you off," which Ted took to mean that he would be removed from the home. As a child and adolescent, he believed that any mistake he made could trigger "tragic" results. In response, Ted gave up any urge toward being rebellious; his approach to his father was as a supplicant: "Please don't leave me outside."

Much later, when Ted had asked his father why he threatened him this way, he explained that it was a means of discipline he had heard a friend describe, and it seemed to work. Of course his choice of such measures, and his callous explanation of them, had to do with his own parenting. Ted's paternal grandfather, a rigid Prussian and an M.D., had put great pressure on Ted's father to become an M.D. also. Feeling both unable and unwilling to respond to this demand, Ted's father turned in other directions, working as an actor in his 20s and eventually going into manufacturing. During Ted's youth, his father had consistently lied about his own life story, embellishing it with accounts of academic degrees, experiences, and possessions that he had never really acquired. After he started therapy, Ted contacted his father's siblings and discovered that each, in one way or another, expressed a dread of not achieving according to the grandfather's demands. The others were appalled at Ted when he tried to talk to them about one uncle he found living out of a suitcase in a rundown boarding house. Here was one member of the family upon whom doomsday had fallen with a solid crunch; the others could not bear to hear about it.

It had seemed natural to Ted's father, in turn, to impose harsh demands. When he watched Ted play ball, he would confine his commentary to the strikeout or the muffed catch, never mentioning the run earned. He was opposed to Ted's marriage, as if Ted were a traitor to go through with it. The day Ted's first son was born, Ted's father met him at the hospital and, without clarification, announced, "I can't take much more of this fighting, you are killing me." Three weeks later, he was dead of a heart attack.

To conceive of Ted's "doomsday panic" simply as a one-to-one transference response, originating in his experience with his father, would be to miss the dynamics at work here. Ted's mother played a crucial part in a three-way process. While Ted was in the elementary grades, she reviewed and corrected all his homework, criticized his handwriting, and scolded him liberally for not doing better work. While Ted was in high school, his mother interceded for him with school authorities on various occasions and even took over the task of getting rid of an unwanted girlfriend. There was some speculation among Ted's friends that when Ted went to college, his mother would take an apartment off campus.

In response to his mother's interventions, Ted never dared flare up because she always stood up to his father for him, and Ted felt that she was his safety net, necessary to his survival. When his mother took Ted's side against his father, his father would shun the mother too. Ted lived in terror that this precarious equilibrium would collapse, that the moment would finally arrive when his mother, in order to save her marriage, would join forces with his father and throw Ted out in the street.

As Ted described the history of his anxiety, much of it was

related to times when he had suffered from the criticism of a single superior. ''I leave a memo for the boss, I'm just waiting for him to critique it.'' But the real blockbusters, the times when the doomsday panic got hold of him, were times he saw himself as a tiny figure touching off a battle between giants who, when they noticed him, would turn on him and squash him.

The replica of the family pattern in the workplace was vivid enough. But to complete the work with Ted, it was necessary to look also at the origins of his present conviction that he would emerge both as the central figure and as the victim in others' disputes. This fear could have some of its origins in childish egocentricity. But it appeared that the parents chose to fight with each other through him, his father attacking and his mother defending. This would be quite enough to make him the central figure.

Ted's orbit within the family was an uneven one. His father projected on Ted much of the self-disgust he had acquired as a child, without ever going to the extreme of actual banishment. His mother seemed to join with his father in seeing Ted as inadequate, but she offered Ted the hope that if he suffered through the tribulation she prescribed, he could be redeemed. Ted therefore would travel his orbit of despair and redemption, ultimately fearing that if his parents ever got together and agreed on how bad he was, it would spell the end of him. We can speculate, without having the evidence to document it, that Ted's transgressions were unconsciously designed to keep his father's projections focused on Ted and thus divert his father's wrath away from his mother. The need to do so would make Ted a weary traveler around the despair-redemption circuit. In reality the part he played may have helped to give the family whatever stability it had.

The Moderator

Spencer, a business executive in his late 40s, came in because he was depressed about work. Having previously been chief executive officer of a small corporation, he was now in charge of two departments in a large one. This made him feel less important; it bothered him that he did not see "high-level people" as much as he would like. He saw himself as a person who felt worthy as long as he was engaged in a useful dialogue with others. If alone, he would be inclined to have brooding thoughts about all the dragons left unslain.

Spencer saw himself in sharp contrast to his boss. "He's known as difficult to be with. He's brilliant but severe, threatening. He never gives you a warm reception." A comment the boss once made had left Spencer with the impression that he was "not measuring up," although his own analysis of what was going on in his departments led him to think that "I am doing better than he perceives."

The therapist observed that Spencer seemed to be somewhat in awe of his boss. This led Spencer to think about his side of the relationship.

> Maybe I'm too aware of his very high reputation as a manager. It's my nature to be open and respectful. So I don't argue with him as other people would, and maybe he enjoys it when they do. He gives strong, more direct arguments, and I'm more willing to accept his ideas. So that makes me the "weaker sister" and he doesn't think so much of me. That's just the way I am. Maybe I have too much humility.

We have learned over the years to hear the statement, "That's just the way I am," as a declaration of one's position; i.e., "That is the way I am committed to being." This declaration can serve as a massive roadblock in the way of therapeutic movement. Or, if it is explored, it can lead to discoveries about how the client has been pinned down by past designations. In Spencer's case, the therapist felt the critical moment might have come to invite his client to begin to question his designation. Accordingly, the therapist chose a question that would gently extend this invitation, saved for this purpose from a previous session. "You spoke last week about how your boss delays the work?"

Spencer's response showed that he was ready to accept the invitation.

He'll raise a question that needs more homework. He'll go to depths to analyze. So you go back and forth on something that I don't think deserves it. He should have more confidence in his people, to handle it. But I don't say, "John, let me get on with this." You know, if I did say that, I don't think he would say I was out of order.

At this point the therapist moved toward consideration of the family-of-origin system with a question about Spencer's older brother. Spencer replied,

He's a bulldog, more persevering than I am, he'll win by sheer sustained thrust. In my childhood, he and my father were alike in this, so they were always bumping heads together. And I was frequently in the role of Henry Clay, the moderator, the negotiator, the compromiser. I would get them to see something in the other point of view and work something out. Maybe you can compromise too much. I'd talk to father, "Look at brother's situation." I'd talk to brother, "Look at dad's position, you both may have to give more than half to work this out."

Spencer did not know why he had become the moderator, but he knew there would be antagonism in the family if he did not serve in that capacity. And, as he was growing up, he left the role of confronter strictly to his brother.

I never grew into the situation with my father where I'd say, "I'm going to take him on." And that didn't bother me. We worked together on projects. We did many good things together. And I forgot his bad points and remembered what he taught me.

So Spencer could generate warmth in the family through his good relationship with his father, thus offsetting the negatives between his father and brother. The benefits to the family were substantial; not only his brother but also his mother would come to Spencer when they wanted to get his father to do something.

But the cost to Spencer was the splitting off and burying of his own assertiveness; he had little occasion to learn how to assert his own interests in any direct or forceful way. In relation to his boss, he could only fantasize that vigorous action would bring down the kind of wrath that his father visited on his brother. But it did not take long for Spencer to recognize that with his present superior the old ways of relating were simply not going to work. Instead, he was able to begin to glimpse how he and his boss might be able to discuss, or even argue, as peers when the nature of their problems at work called for them to do so.

The Mission

At 32 Agatha found herself so successful at selling mortgage credit for commercial real estate that she was put in charge of training junior members of the credit corporation. This too went well until one day when her supervisor remarked about the lackluster attitude of some of the junior people. Agatha was told to make a pitch for the company that would raise her trainees' level of interest in their jobs. She was well into her first oration on the virtues of the corporation when one of her trainees yawned in her face and she went into a violent, unprecedented anxiety attack that required her to terminate the meeting. The same thing happened a few days later when she was simply showing a job applicant around as a courtesy to the personnel department. Not long afterwards she left her position.

Exploration of antecedents led to the finding that hers was a family in which the father put great pressure on the children to produce intellectually, expressing his displeasure with anything but straight A performance at school and conducting quizzes at the dinner table. Agatha, as the oldest child, not only got the heaviest pressure but also assumed the burden of sometimes telling her father to lay off, taking the brunt of the painful flare-up that might take place. But the heavier burden came when her father, soon after learning he had cancer, became a Christian Scientist and began holding sessions during which he would coach the children to "know the truth" and cast out error. Her father never said he expected them to use their faith healing to cure his cancer, but his desperation was obvious. When he died, Agatha felt a profound sense of failure that went unrecognized and undealt with by the adult world. All that was needed finally to trigger the underlying distress was the sudden sense that she had failed to convey her message of uplift to her trainee group; thus she felt that she had let down both her supervisor and her corporation, just as she felt she had previously let down her father.

Progress in treatment involved helping her reduce her excessively heavy sense of responsibility for her siblings as well as for her surviving parent. Her husband, who had at first been afraid to bring up the subject with her, coached her on how to stop giving them so much advice. This in turn brought relief to and a more cordial response from her siblings. The special beneficiary was her husband, whose own anxiety symptoms abated as Agatha reduced her continual angry displacement upon him of her frustration about giving up work. Finally, she began considering whether she might be able to find another good job.

Apathy

In Chapter 1 we described Mark, whose promotion led to such apathy that his company had initiated outplacement procedures. In his case, the promotion meant that he had to delegate everything that had been of interest to him. What stimulated Mark's interests throughout his life tended to be associated with his mother and her interests. It seems probable that Mark unconsciously perceived the promotion, like some prior events in his life, as a move by his father to pull him away from his mother; in this event his apathy would signify his loyalty to his mother, and the outplacement work would signify nothing more than the beginning of another frustrating round of self-canceling efforts.

THE EFFECTS OF FAMILY PATTERNS

The people whom we have just described brought their family baggage to work with them. We are confident that other methods of data gathering, such as sensitive on-site observations backed up by retrospective interviews, could tell us much more about the effects of family-of-origin designation on how people work and how they relate in the workplace.

The Vertical and Horizontal Dimensions

In these cases, it is relevant to cite the observation made by McGoldrick and Carter (1982) having to do with the intersection of vertical and horizontal stress as a point where anxiety can be expected to peak. Vertical stresses are those impinging on the present from the past, especially the intergenerational pressures that we are calling designation. Horizontal stresses are those occurring in the here and now, like the expectations of a supervisor or of co-workers. For example, in the case of Susan (p. 54) who came into therapy with a somewhat muted complaint about her trouble in talking to people, it became evident that she was caught between the restrictions of the past and the requirements of the present; the result was expressed as a crisis in her confidence about herself.

The carry-over of patterns from the family into the workplace has significance not only for the individual to whom this baggage belongs, but also for the organization itself, which provides a fertile soil for such transplants and tends to pattern its own functioning upon them.

THE READINESS TO PERFORM

The ways administrators function depend heavily on their perceptions of how people are motivated. Drucker (1974), for instance, presenting the hazards of flexibility in organizations, endorses the proposition that a large proportion of people are "weak, vulnerable, timid, and impaired"(p. 526), hence unable to carry the responsibility that is thrust upon them in a flexible organization. Such an outlook can shape the way people treat other people at work.

We adhere to an alternative point of view, having to do with the nature of people's potential. Our view is based on our clinical experience that if we understand the patterns that people are designated to bring from home to work with them, we can usually help those people to make shifts, sometimes quite dramatic shifts, from how "weak, vulnerable, timid, and impaired" they appear to be. Drawing on experience with a variety of client populations, including some who were heavily drug-dependent, we would advance the general proposition that, with due allowance for such factors as constitutionally given energy level and intelligence, the degree of immobilization people present is a measure of the extent of the immobilizing messages they have received. Somewhere under the pileup of prohibitions there is usually a person who still has enough strength left to struggle to get out from under. The administrator who finds it easy to regard people as "weak, vulnerable, timid, and impaired" is engaging in heavy collusion with voices from the past.

While any attempt at a typology would be premature and misleading, we present here a loosely arranged sequence of examples, drawn mostly from this book, for the purpose of illustrating how family designations can affect the freedom of a person to commit him- or herself to work. The sequence begins with instances of designations that can lead to failure, and continues on to those that can lead to partial or full success. The first example is that of the person whose parents have consistently made the prediction that he or she is going to be a failure. Other family members may join in giving this message, achieving a false sense of solidarity by isolating one person who is designated as no good. This is sometimes made more concrete by identifying the designated person with someone else in the family who has already failed.

The prediction of failure may disguise the parents' wish for the person to remain home and be caretaker, a wish that may be presented in other ways than by predicting failure. The essence of the designation is, your energies belong at home. The designated person may arrange to carry out this mission by presenting him- or herself to the world as a person riddled with phobic anxieties. Or the covert caretaker may engage in an angry refusal to behave at work in conformance with expectations, thereby losing a job and gaining an excuse to go home.

The injunction to fail is destructive in its intent; the injunction to be caretaker may carry some promise of return benefits, but its effect may still be quite destructive. Somewhat less destructive yet potentially immobilizing is the message from the family to "lie low so you do not expose us to risk." All the siblings may get the same message, or one sibling may be selected as the risk taker while the next one is put on standby and told to play it safe, so the family will have a replacement in case the first one gets lost, or so the parents' internal conflicts can get played out by having their children play contradictory roles.

A little further along in our sample is the person whose invisible loyalty to an incompetent parent mandates that he or she endure a dreary lifetime of being chained to the slow chariots of incompetent supervisors. This person is always committed to looking at least one degree more "weak, vulnerable, timid, and impaired" than the supervisor, a role for which there is often a reinforcing payoff.

A bit further along is the person who defers to others out of fear of replicating the behavior of a cruel and domineering parent. Such an individual may make a valuable contribution to an organization while remaining a shadowy figure.

Next comes the individual who has been taught that he or she must defer to an older sibling who is regarded as the rightful heir or heiress. The presumption is that the older one has both superior rights and superior powers, and the younger one may learn to settle for a subordinate role.

A little further on is a large cluster of people whose parents have urged them to go out and compete while covertly stressing that it would be just as well not to show any signs of outdistancing the mother or father en route. What may look on the surface like genuine moves toward autonomy may in fact be the transfer of dependencies from home to workplace. As they did with their teachers at school and college, these people may invest a good deal of energy in figuring out how to get on the good side of their supervisors and stay there; the supervisors may love it, even while complaining of their subordinates' lack of drive. These individuals may be able to do good work, but their anxiety about how they stand with the boss may be a constant deterrent to their taking initiative. Unless they are lucky, or unless they receive some kind of jolt in life that impels them to do further work on the quality of their relationships, they may make a collective contribution to bureaucratic inertia.

Less committed to a fixed role, and therefore having their potential more readily available, are the individuals who received ambivalent messages from a parent. An oldest daughter, for instance, might stand in for a sick mother, being relegated to child status again whenever mother recovered enough to resume control. Such a person might feel high anxiety about relationships with supervisors and peers, complaining that he or she was not given enough authority to do the job, yet continually striving for a higher position.

A similarly placed group includes those who are struggling with contradictory designations from their parents, e.g., a message from the mother to be artistic conflicting with a message from the father to be practical. One of these messages may carry the person quite a distance before he or she collides with the other message and stops short.

Also capable of traveling a considerable distance is the person, usually a woman, whose family demanded that she be available to them, yet did not even show enough interest in what she did outside to set up any proscriptions. Such a person may engage in a good deal of horizontal movement, achieving quite well in one field before discovering that it yields no satisfaction, because it was not seeded by parental approval, and moving on to search somewhere else.

Somewhere past the mid-range of our sequence is the individual whose childhood isolation in a family managed by depressive, distancing parents has left him or her feeling that it is mandatory to remain invisible; this person may feel no restraints about doing work of very high quality, yet expect to be overlooked and so take no steps toward getting recognized. If supervisors and peers make moves to penetrate the person's isolation, this may generate considerable anxiety, but the outcome can be a productive one.

Capable of swift travel, but vulnerable to sometimes crippling anxiety attacks as well as failure to make use of opportunities, is the person whose parents provided strong messages about achieving, yet used his or her mistakes as occasions for major blowups during which various demons might be let loose, such as the parent's bitterness toward each other and themselves for their own failures.

Moving further, we find the individual who during childhood became parent by default to his or her own parents, learning to function with a heavy sense of responsibility, and eventually pushing on to a high level of achievement accompanied by a high level of anxiety. Such a person might feel compelled to challenge the incompetence of a superior, sometimes with disastrous results. The degree of anxiety implicit in the person's drive might also impel him or her to come down too harshly on subordinates.

Performing at a high level, but sometimes with a driven quality that throws their lives off balance, are people who have found the means to carry out a strong mandate to succeed. This could be a directive to succeed for a father who failed, stand in for a father or sibling who died, or carry the family banner of success into the next generation. Some of these people may have been more successful at manipulating the image of success than at actually producing anything, but to the world at large it will appear that they have accomplished their mission. Inwardly they may feel that they have missed the mark, that what they have done does not come out of their own "soul"; or the success, even though driven by a family mandate, may bring genuine satisfaction.

Whatever the cost to the individual to get on top, the cost to those around the achiever may be very substantial. The achiever whose own father was hostile and distancing may displace his or her revenge on subordinates, reveling in the perception of them as weak people who are not to be trusted. The would-be fast-tracker, charged by narcissistic parents with the mandate to get ahead at all costs, may regard the home as a "pitstop," staying put just long enough to get refreshed and refueled and draining all the other family members in the process. As an added treat, he or she may subject other family members to paroxysms of narcissistic rage if they leave obstacles in the path.

This sample, finally, would not be complete without reference to the substantial group of people whose families have left the track open for them, who feel comfortable in the environment of the workplace, who feel a competitive urge to use whatever abilities they have been given, and who move up without evidence of major struggle because for them it seems like the natural thing to do.

5

The Impact of Family Patterns on Work Systems

We can assume that business and family systems evolved from the same original roots; certainly the merchants' guilds and their apprentice system had elements in common with family structure, and long before that, tribal structure provided a basic model. To a significant degree, business and family systems contain common elements, a fact that has implications for the way they each function. And their interaction supports the implications. But it would be a basic mistake to assume that the principles of one can be successfully transferred over to guide the operation of the other. And, an examination with its focus limited to either metaphoric or actual similarities would miss the understanding to be gained from an exploration of the significant differences between workplace and family systems.

LOGIC

Parents may spell out rules for family functioning, but this is nothing like the logic required to run a business. In keeping with the logic of the organization chart, parts of a business may be added, removed, or shifted about if the moves are justified by the "bottom line." The whole structure can be revised beyond recognition, without a great deal of thought to the "human components," whose lives are touched by every decision. This is the logic of the machine, not the logic of the family, and it is evident that there are times when the logic of such rearrangements takes on a life of its own, without being traceable to a human source: "It's what the *company* wants." Eric Erikson (1968), speaking of man's identification with the machine, suggested that we have a desperate need to function smoothly and cleanly, to limit or nullify human error. In their efforts to make the organization chart look smooth and clean, the corporate decision-makers may fall out of touch with the actual effects of their moves at the working level. Making one unit subordinate to another, for instance, may mean that a highly qualified person must now accept the arbitrary decisions of another person who is unprepared to make them. While parents and children sometimes make arbitrary decisions on matters affecting each other's welfare, the family as a whole cannot be arbitrarily restructured by absentee authorities.

RUPTURE OF RELATIONSHIPS

The impact of business logic can take precedence over the preservation of relationships. Basic to family structure is continuity, a chain stretching back in time. The people who form this chain create a synergism of interests that is often too complex to be put into any verbal formula. It can be expressed through values, attitudes, ways of dealing with each other, and ways of dealing with the world. A member of this chain can be rejected; but this is only a different (and sometimes tighter) kind of binding; there is no such thing as being laid off or fired. Even when a family member dies, he or she lives on in the memories of others as a part of the family, with a place established by rituals and mourning. Some families deteriorate, but a family cannot be signed out of existence.

In business it is possible for a strong synergism of interests to be forged between co-workers through years of association, but these bonds can be broken overnight, either through the depar-

ture of individuals or through the closing down or reorganiza-
tion of the business. Since this potential for disruption of relationships does not exist in the family, people have no basic pattern
to fall back on for dealing with it. What they have learned about
breakup of friendships, teams, and classes at school may not have
prepared them for anything as stressful as the losses involved
in dismissals or reassignments at work, where so much of people's lives may be at stake. If the stress of change is severe
enough, the only coping pattern available from the family repertoire may be the family pattern for coping with death. If, in their
attempts to deal with their distress around being dismissed or
seeing others dismissed, people do fall back on such patterns,
bringing into play such defenses as denial, enmeshment, rigid
adherence to artificially imposed structure, etc., the results for
both the people and for the business may be costly.

LOYALTY

Though they may not be consistently acknowledged or acted
upon, loyalties within the family are reciprocal. Loyalty in the
workplace, on the other hand, is not often reciprocal, in spite of
the lip service it is given. Management may say, "We take care
of our people," and point at pension plans, company cars, etc.
But this coexists with a strong conviction at management level
that the competitive survival and success of the company take
priority over everything else. Accordingly, the security net may
be arbitrarily withdrawn, yet most employees live day-by-day in
a state of denial that this can happen. In fact, many employees
would say that they "take a lot of crap" *in exchange for the security.*
Where does this piece of illogic come from? We believe it is a
direct carry-over of the early sense that, "As long as I do my part
in the family, I'm secure." This denial can coexist with other
defensive maneuvers that impair the effectiveness of the individual and of the company.

However, the employee may feel some freedom to leave regardless of how deeply committed he or she is to the job. The
period of adjustment for new people cannot truly be based on

any expectations about permanence. It is not often acknowledged that this is a kind of marriage that must end in divorce. We believe that the more effort people unconsciously exert in becoming enmeshed in familylike systems in business, the less prepared they will be to deal with often unpleasant pieces of reality like this.

ACCOUNTABILITY AND SHAME

Acts that would never be tolerated from an individual, even acts that could send a person to prison, are often excused, whitewashed, or even applauded when performed in the name of the company. In families, by contrast, shameful acts reverberate through the generations, often with debilitating consequences. When a father is hauled off to trial and jail for the rape of the neighbor, the son will be left with a limited and most unattractive range of responses. If he suppresses his memory of the event, this suppression could have a marked effect on his future behavior toward his father and others. If he tries to deny the implications of the event, this could contribute to the formation of a character disorder, the effects of which might impair the lives of his children if it did not destroy him. Or throughout his life he could carry a burden of shame that would undermine each of his efforts, and probably his relationships too, and could intrude into the lives of grandchildren and great-grandchildren and perhaps beyond. Or, in an act of perverted loyalty, he could go out and rape his neighbor and reconnect with dear old dad in jail.

In the family, an exploitative, corrupt, or disgraceful act sends out shock waves that blast the immediate family and can rattle every relative, even those who are living their lives at a considerable distance. A great-uncle's suicide can change the way the world feels, much as we might try to deny its effect. And the shock waves roll on through time, reaching down through the generations with subtle yet pervasive power.

But in an organization, the individual is, with some notable exceptions, permitted and even expected to function with diminished personal responsibility, perhaps in repayment for having offered his or her allegiance to an amorphous, impersonal master. A corporation can be so vast that, except for the few in the top positions, its employees are oblivious to and untouched by corporate actions that, personally, they would deem reprehensible. "I didn't know anything about it," said an ecologically aware young executive from Mobil Oil, when asked how he felt about his company's having been caught dumping toxic drilling fluids into the already endangered ecosystems of the Cook Inlet in Alaska and Mobile Bay in Alabama. Morale can be temporarily affected when corporate malfeasance is brought to light, and some highly principled individuals might resign, but internal public-relations campaigns and management rationalizations can soon bring things back to "business as usual."

Accordingly, in the area of personal accountability and responsibility, the company more closely resembles a nation than a family, demanding loyalty and the fulfillment of certain key obligations while offering to cloak, with personal anonymity and distance, actions the individual might never think to undertake on his own. A DuPont worker might be appalled by the fact that the Occupational Safety and Health Administration has listed his company among the eight worst violators of worker safety in the chemical industry, just as a citizen of Iran might be appalled by his country's taking hostages, each without for a second taking personal responsibility or feeling shame.

OVERLAP OF FUNCTION

Regardless of similarities, there is also an inherent difference in the way families and businesses are organized. In a family there can be two "psychological parents," with much natural overlap of function. If the parents are immobilized, a grandfather or an aunt may pinch-hit. The overlapping causes confusion but it also provides enrichment. In business, by contrast, as Lawrence and Lorsch (1969) have pointed out, there is a need to differentiate the functions of different units, and if the structure gets complicated there may have to be units to coordinate other units. Business logic requires that overlap be avoided as much as possible. Similar attempts to differentiate within the family may lead to clarity about functioning, yet result in each member's being out of touch with crucial aspects of the family's life; e.g., the working father can easily lose track of his children's school progress if that is seen as the mother's province.

Differentiating Between Family and Business

Unless the individual is alert to the differences between family systems and work systems, he or she will be vulnerable to the continual undertow of temptation to regard work as an extension of family, to snuggle into a cocoon that seems familiar but that in reality can be rudely ripped away. The cost to the company that fosters this kind of reenactment may be the loss of the person's potential. The cost to the person may be not only the loss of potential for autonomous output, but the failure or partial failure of individuation. Bernstein (1985) reports that her interviews with corporate personnel bear out her own impressions about the carry-over of behavior from family to business, yet some of her examples show how different business can be from family. According to Bernstein, a company "father" may select a company "son" or "daughter," upon whom he will lavish affection and offer special individual guidance, the quid pro quo being allegiance. But let the "son" or "daughter" stray once from loyalty or ignore "father's" advice on more than one occasion, and the relationship dissolves and a new heir or heiress is brought forward. By contrast, in an actual family nothing can alter the fact that a father and child are related. In ordinary circumstances, a child passing through adolescence may leave in his or her wake years of turmoil, of extreme displeasure on every side; yet it is the rare case when this displeasure finally eventuates in a complete break. Home, by definition, is where they always have to let you in. A young person whose quest for a separate self led him or her constantly to disregard the father's advice indeed might be in for a very rude awakening if he or she attempted to continue this pattern with a "company father," as one of our clients ruefully reported.

Having drawn attention to crucial distinctions between family and business, we move now to consideration of important aspects of overlap.

The Ascent

The notion of vertical structure in business is usually presented as logic, but in reality it is mixed up with a bundle of very powerful metaphors that relate to family. As already noted, vertical business structure has something in common with, and carries strong connotations of, the intergenerational structure of the family. "Looking up" is what one did for many years when the parents were physically bigger and one yearned to catch up. Levinson (1978, p. 59) adopts the well-known metaphor of the ladder to talk about getting up in the world; he uses it to refer to "all dimensions of advancement," including income, power, fame, and creativity. The person who is "making it" is "climbing the ladder." Sometimes we may glance down to see if our safety net is in place beneath. And when things go wrong, businessmen hope to soften the fall with a "golden parachute." But this patent logic of the vertical structure may have even less impact on organizations than do the emotions, sometimes quite primitive, having to do with vertical relationships.

Transference. Such metaphors as those above have a profound effect on the way we look at and feel about our working world. "Looking up" at the person above in the hierarchy is an image that serves to trigger transference responses. And transference responses are usually *exaggerations*. The child's unconscious memory of the parent is not a recollection of how the parent actually behaved; it is a memory of the child's *fantasy* about the parent. If the parent sometimes behaved like a minor-league ogre, the child-now-grown will most likely have a lurking internalized image of a world-class ogre, and this image can be mobilized by certain behaviors of the boss.

The intergenerational clashes of value that occurred between child and parent are also likely to occur between different generations of management, and the current clash is likely to be pre-heated by the old feelings from the family. The parent-child tensions stirred by parents' fears of obsolescence will come back to provide a haunting note in relations between junior and senior executives. The subtle or not so subtle tug-of-war over the position of authority is played out again at work; and again the feelings that were generated in the family over this issue will be aroused.

As we have suggested already in Chapter 4, reactivation of transference in the business setting is not likely to be a simple one-to-one affair; instead, reactivation of the most dominant aspect of the family system is likely to bring with it some degree of reactivation of the system as a whole. Levinson (1978), for instance, speaks of the tendency at work to think of men several years older as "older siblings." Wetzel (1984) observes that no developmental era is ever totally relinquished, so everyone is psychologically pulled toward earlier phases. In those earlier phases, the embrace of the family was likely to be a dominant aspect of life. And as we observed in Chapter 4, there are likely to be plenty of people around at work who will stand in for family members to help reactivate the old family drama.

Triangles. The metaphor of the ladder does not immediately suggest anything about triangles. But suppose there was a man on a ladder, and above him another man, and below him a third. Suppose the man on top reached down with his foot and tapped the fingers of the man in the middle. What would the man in the middle be likely to do then? We believe he would be very likely to move down a rung, and if the fingers of the man beneath were on that rung, then a triangle is created.

The vertical hierarchy, in other words, is a natural setup for triangles. McGoldrick and Carter (1982), in drawing their distinction between the vertical and horizontal dimensions, suggest that the vertical flow includes transgenerational patterns that are transmitted primarily through the mechanism of emotional triangling. Bowen (1978) talks about the value of a person's being individuated enough to stay out of triangles. In the situation we are discussing, the man in the middle cannot simply disappear from the ladder and let the man on top have it out with the man on the bottom. Rather than getting out of a triangle, the task may be how to avoid setting up a triangle. This can be difficult; it is easier to respond to the stresses from a superior by passing them along to a subordinate. We are accustomed to hearing the phrase, "the buck stops here," in connection with passing problems *up* a line of command. It is usually an unsung hero who is capable of making the buck stop on its way *down*.

It seems that triangling has profound implications for people in organizations and therefore for the organizations themselves. Triangles seem to be adapted to passing stresses downwards and also to blocking communication upwards. The senior author was at one time involved in a study of the effects of management behavior on the functioning of a foreman (Ulrich, Booz, & Lawrence, 1950). It seemed as if the foreman would be caught forever in a triangle between his managers and the employees on the assembly line. The company was scrambling for a share of the new market in transistors, the manufacturing procedures were still semi-experimental, and the managers were acutely unhappy about what they perceived as the bumbling and indifferent performance of the workers, upon whom the romance of transistors was lost as they tried to get the pesky little things to stick together right. Giving vent to his frustration, the general manager said, "The employees have a responsibility for telling us what is on their minds and we have a responsibility for telling them what we are thinking. They don't tell us and they won't listen." In fact the employees had plenty to say, but they said it to the foreman, who would, if he thought about it at all, never have considered such material suitable for the ears of management. Deprived of this input, what the management thought about the workers contained as much fantasy as fact, and the managers tended to behave accordingly. The workers' reactions to this behavior were thus misinterpreted, and so on in an endless dysfunctional cycle.

The foreman was not only aware of but also sensitive to the employees' feelings about the job, and his treatment of them often showed his consideration for those feelings. But there were times when the pressures from above grew severe enough so that the foreman felt he must put on a display of forceful action. At such times, he found himself deserting the role of holding an umbrella over the employees; instead he found himself holding a whip over them. His unceasing zigzags back and forth, from joining with the workers to joining with the management, left him in a chronic state of moderately agitated semi-exhaustion.

The manager-supervisor-employee triangle is not, of course, the only kind of triangle that can occur in the organizational setting. A triangle can be formed between a supervisor and two subordinates, between an employee, a supervisor, and a staff member from an adjunctive department, between a subordinate, a manager, and an official from the headquarters office, any two people and an outside consultant, etc.

These observations suggest how triangular relationships can serve to block vital communication upwards in the organizational setting, while making people suffer severe inter- and intrapersonal tension. A complicating factor is that the triangles in business are usually given the weight of protocol, which serves further to constrict the flow of information. For instance, the rule that one must not bypass a superior is often taken to mean that one cannot have *any* direct communication with the people above; the superior is *expected* to get in between. Our navy acquaintance, whose ties to home brought him mention in Chapter 4, had an anecdote that graphically illustrates this rule.

> As a young lieutenant jg, I was once called up to the bridge of our aircraft carrier, which happened to be the flagship so we had the admiral on board. The ship's gunnery officer stood between me and the admiral. He relayed the admiral's questions about aviation ordnance to me and relayed my answers, badly garbled, back. Never mind that there was a war on; it evidently would have been bad form for the admiral to permit a junior grade lieutenant to address him directly. And I think the gunnery officer was afraid of being left out.

Of course, the triangles in business organizations were not transplanted there from the family. Triangles have their own indigenous growth wherever there are three people, each of whom cannot handle his or her end of two one-to-one relationships. But the relevance of family is that the way people behave in triangles anywhere is most likely to be determined by the way they behaved in the triangles in their family of origin. What is more, we believe that what made people act as they did within their family triangles was quite likely to be determined by such factors as legacy and designation. The opportunities for replay of these behaviors are boundless.

The restriction of information flow, as in the two examples above, means that management often makes major operating and policy decisions in a vacuum. It also means that over time management can become myopic or even blind to the impact of its actions and decisions on lower echelons. Consequently, when lower echelons react critically to management action, management perceives the response as being due to extraneous factors, e.g., faults in an individual employee, disloyalty, performance failure, outside agitators, etc., and then management behaves again according to the misperception.

The downwards transmission of stress. We mentioned above that as well as blocking communication upwards, triangles tend to become a vehicle for transmission of stress downwards. It is generally understood that top management sets the pace in these matters, and that the only effective avenue toward change is through changes in top management.

Much is being said currently about corporate "culture" and "style." The "culture," as Schein (1978) points out, may be determined partly by whether the top people come from production, sales, or finance. The culture, considered to be an amalgam of beliefs, values, and rituals, may have a distinctive tone. In one corporation, the tone was one of adventure; new technological breakthroughs were awaited with excitement and highly rewarded, while failed efforts were not penalized.

Corporate culture cannot be readily distinguished from corporate style, which also tends to be defined by the way the top managers function. DeVries and Miller (1984) describe how the style or personality of the chief executive officer may have an impact on how the company functions; e.g., if the chief is grandiose, unduly cautious and suspicious, or depressive, the attitude of the whole company may reflect this posture. In one corporation with which we had contact, the chief executive officer set such an example of macho toughness that the only subordinates who could stick with him were ones who were well-versed in the art of sadomasochism, and the organization was known for the level of tension under which its employees operated.

DeVries (1984) suggests how contagious the behavior of a senior executive can be, and how devastating its effects on his subordinates and his organization. DeVries extends the term "folie à deux" (p. 157) to characterize this phenomenon, i.e., the sharing of a delusional system by two or more individuals. It seems clear that a process of triangulation is involved here, the third individual coming in to pick up the "contagion" from the first two.

The culture or style serves not only to transmit systems of attitudes and values, it is part of an emotional ambiance in which stress also can be very rapidly communicated down through the hierarchy. Wiseman (1982) applies Bowen's concepts of emotional process to the problem of stress in corporations. For instance, if disturbing events such as a sudden shift in the market, or personal illness in executives' families, generate a burst of anxiety at the top of the hierarchy, this can rapidly be transmitted downwards throughout the organization, via the triangle. If the anxiety is severe and persistent enough, the complications can become enormous. Ill-founded and capricious decision-making may be one of the consequences; an atmosphere rampant with destructive gossip is another; the long list continues and may include diminished worker satisfaction, decreased production, subgroup conflict, misuse of authority, role confusion, projection, scapegoating, sexual acting-out between employees, and substance abuse.

Concerning the question of how emotionality is transmitted, Bowen (1978) observes that emotional issues in administrative organizations have the "same basic patterns" as emotional issues in the family. We can say that when a chief executive officer overflows with anxiety, much of it is likely to spill out on the person directly below in the hierarchy, who as we have noted is less likely to contain it than to let it spill out onto the people beneath. Also, a period of heightened anxiety is one in which transference reactions are more likely to be triggered; and, as we have observed, transference reactions are exaggerations, so that the subordinates are likely to amplify the magnitude of whatever is going on.

While anxiety may be the more readily observable phenomenon, in the undercurrent of corporate life flows substantial fear, as the security guards can attest who have had to track missing executives down to hideouts in hotel rooms, where they had sought to pickle their terror in alcohol. One man told about the shock of stunned disbelief that ran through a department meeting when, in response to the general manager's asking, "Are there any questions?" he shouted from the back of the room, "*Yeah, when do I get a chance at promotion?*" His co-workers would not let go of the incident for months afterwards. Commenting on their reaction, our man observed, "It is the essence of life to cover your ass." Fear of doomsday at work, as we have already observed, can have its roots in the fear of doomsday in the family. Not only do the emotional issues at work have the same basic patterns as the emotional issues in the family, but also there is really not a great deal to prevent emotional currents at work from reactivation old emotional currents from the families of the workers. The undercurrent of fear is part of the emotionality that intrudes on rational process.

The attempt to deny these feelings, to keep them from surfacing, is strong. One company set the policy that any employee who started to cry for any reason was to be sent home for the day. For an executive to cry at work is usually unthinkable. In the absence of means provided within corporations for coping with emotion, people naturally fall back upon their repertoire of family behaviors. In later sections, we will have more to say about the methods that people bring with them from home for coping with fear and what impact this has on organizations.

The recurrence of a basic tension. In Chapter 3 we suggested that throughout almost the whole of life there is tension between the kinds of usefulness a family designates for a person and the kinds of productive striving a person tries to define for him- or herself. This tension between self and family is extended into adult life, and we see that the conditions of the workplace enable the re-creation of this tension between the individual and the work hierarchy of which he or she is a part. As the individual ascends the ladder, the conditions of the ascent seem familiar; i.e., how the people further up the ladder define one's usefulness to them may, for the reasons we have been reviewing, be quite out of synchronization with how usefulness is defined for oneself. So a person can easily be getting it from both sides at once, from the family and from the workplace, on how to be useful; and somewhere in the middle the person on his or her way to individuating may be seeking a ''zone of spontaneity,'' a space where he or she can call the tune.

The Here and Now

Production on the horizontal dimension. In Chapter 4 we referred to the distinction drawn by McGoldrick and Carter (1982) between the vertical dimension (intergenerational) and the horizontal dimension (the here and now). It seems to us that whereas organization charts involve vertical dimension and all its connotations, the spontaneous productive efforts of individuals, or of individuals linked together in groups, can best be conceptualized as taking place in the *here and now*. In other words, such efforts are occurring on the horizontal dimension. As Peters and Waterman (1982) stated, ''We have come to believe that the key success factor in business is simply getting one's arms around almost any practical problem and knocking it off—now'' (p. 126).

Organization chart, present tense. If we were to make up an organization chart based on organizational style that could make some sense to the individual who was trying to cultivate his or her own ways of being productive, the units actually responsible for design and production would be arranged horizontally across the top, and all other units, including the office of the chief executive officer (CEO), would be arranged around them in such a way as to indicate that these other units existed to facilitate the work of the units designing and making the product. One might, for example, do the chart like a stage, with the production units arrayed across it, the finance and purchasing people in the wings, the sales people out in the box office, and the CEO coordinating everything from the center of the orchestra pit.

Of course, we realize the above has a certain unreality in that it focuses on production and worker productivity as if these were or should be the true goals of business. In the "real" world, the business of business is making money, and so the finance department must share center stage with production, not only to oversee cost effectiveness but to harness the inherent power of money to make money. Finance departments function under the guidance and wisdom of the cliché "the rich get richer," and for the most part they are staffed by people who have developed knowledge and skills that have little or nothing to do with the making and marketing of the product, even though it serves as the wellspring for the money they manage. The chief financial officer of Proctor and Gamble, for instance, along with his entire staff, could go to Ford or General Electric tomorrow without being overly concerned about the differences between wash-day products, cars, or appliances. And more and more, the same can be said for those in other areas of the business world, where specialization seems to have become the key to success. Managers of marketing, human resources, public relations, even top administrators, seem comfortable taking their knowledge and skill not only from company to company but from one industry to another. In the business world, it would be considered naive to wonder aloud about the similarities and differences between soda and computers in response to news that the chief executive officer of Pepsi has taken over the top slot at Apple. But who is left to mind the store or to take personal pride in the product? We believe such specialization, with its splitting off of functions and values from one another, accounts for much of the current uncertainty and bewilderment that aspiring young business people express about their efforts in the workplace.

The "zone of spontaneity." As we noted in Chapter 4, Drucker (1974) presents the thesis that many people are too weak to be able to work without direction. Of course, people vary in the degree to which they are free to commit themselves to work, as our sequence of cases in Chapter 4 indicated. Some will feel highly anxious outside of tight parameters; some will be anxious if they cannot be in a position of control, and a certain proportion will be far enough along on the way to individuation so that they will find some measure of autonomy to be a welcome challenge. How these people respond at work will also, of course, depend on the nature of the supervisor. One whose heavy-handed and negative approach stunts growth may be tolerated longer by those who are not ready to overcome their own dependencies. A supervisor who has some skill in sizing up the degree of responsibility a subordinate is ready to take will probably get a positive response. How well the supervisor handles the task of allocating responsibility will also depend, of course, on the degree of support he or she enjoys from the top officers of the company.

Let us look a little further into the question of what it means for a person to be productive, to bring resources from within to interact with the external environment and create something of value. The type of production line that can be operated by robots does not, of course, invite the individual to bring out something from inside, and it is fortunate that most kinds of work, whether calling primarily for manual or mental effort, do not dictate to the worker exactly how to respond. A person is not likely to perform a task exactly the same way twice, because he or she will have begun making adjustments, perhaps very minute ones, and perhaps not altogether conscious ones either, to the cues coming from the job. If we look at an operation seemingly as simple and concrete as a woodcutter using a chain saw, there are, metaphorically speaking, active dialogues occurring among the person on the saw, the saw itself, and the tree. The tree is giving cues to the saw, the saw is passing them on with its own variations into the hands and arms of the woodcutter, and the woodcutter is responding in all kinds of ways, coming from within him- or herself. These ways can include feelings of being in close control, of strength, or of fatigue; being keenly attuned to the sound and vibration and weight of the saw, sensing whether it needs to be tuned or sharpened, how it is proceeding into the cut, and above all how close the tree is to falling. There will be a time of suspense as the moment approaches for the tree to convey its first tremor.

We are not the first ones to use this metaphor, of course, but through it we want to convey the fact that as this process of gathering cues and making adjustments gains momentum, what can take place is an intuitive leap to a new grasp of the work. This response seems to come from deep inside the person, beyond logical thought. It usually has something to do with right-brain functioning, and its result may be described as skill, creativity, ingenuity, or innovativeness. We believe it can take place in any work situation where the necessary conditions have been set up for the worker to function without excessive control. The cumulative effect of these intuitive reactions can be an increase in the quality and the quantity of output. The efforts of outside experts may be required at various points to improve the process, but quality control as a process imposed from outside cannot take the place of the quality control that is generated by the worker—when it is accepted by management that the worker can often be the best authority on the job.

The intuitive process we are describing here can also occur in groups, as resonance builds among the responses of the group members. For groups to be able to operate spontaneously and draw on intuition, they have to be small and they cannot afford to have a formal organization. Peters and Waterman (1982) cite academic findings that teams are more productive when they are small, consist of volunteers, exist for a limited time, and set their own goals. These authors describe what they classify as "skunk works," i.e., small, flexible groups or individuals who achieve more by working *outside* the regular system, literally taking their work to a dingy loft or to somebody's basement. In order for this to happen, of course, the regular system has to "leak" a little, i.e., some kind of overt or covert permission has to be given. According to these authors, such a group can sometimes make out better than corporate engineering teams composed of hundreds of people. In one case, a "skunk works" member took home with him two samples of a major corporate product that had "bombed," and after three weeks of tinkering he came back with a successful product.

Other authors have produced similar observations. Naisbitt (1982) mentions "high touch" quality control circles, that is, groups of workers who discuss work-related problems and solutions. Wetzel (1984) discusses the value of autonomous work teams.

Such groups, to be effective, tend to consist of peers, people of roughly equal authority who are well enough individuated so any age differences in the group will not get in the way. To paraphrase Wetzel (1984), work environments that are autonomous, nonhierarchical, and egalitarian are both economically and socially rewarding.

Anyone who has been closely associated with such a group will be aware of the intensity of effort that goes along with the pressure of meeting the deadline. We have observed that cohesive working groups may, as stress increases, show a seemingly infinite capacity to match their tempo to the demands of the job, until the demands are met. In one instance, a group of officials from New York who were visiting one of their paper mills in Maine complained because the men just seemed to be loafing around their machine. Each machine was an enormous structure, occupying the length of a factory room, designed to take in pulp at one end and turn out great rolls of paper at the other. In reply to the owners' complaint, the manager ignored his men; instead, he stepped over and brought the back of his hand down on the edge of the paper as it raced through the machine. The paper instantly tore across, and chaos erupted within the machine as partially made paper started looping in all directions and jamming the rollers. Within the same instant, the men were at their stations and running through the intricate moves they and the men before them had devised to clear and reset the works. The mill manager knew what his men could do, and we believe he was able to share in the pride they felt in the procedures they had created. Once the job was done, they were back loafing again, all without a word. To the New York people, the manager said only, "They were working, but we weren't making paper." No further defense of his men was needed.

A basis in trust. For groups to be free to function, it is implicit that a measure of trust must exist between the members of the group and the people outside the group who are supporting its functioning. The members must have some confidence that their interests will be protected while they are engrossed in what they are doing, e.g., that they will not be deprived of resources, sidetracked, or dismissed. The support people must be able to enjoy some confidence in the capacity of the group. The track records of the members will have to be considered, but what is also at stake here is whether the support people are *capable* of believing in the capacity of the group.

Outside the family system. We believe that when groups are able to function this way, they have entered the "zone of spontaneity" mentioned earlier. Essential to understanding the structure or functioning of a small peer group is the recognition that the group stands outside the structure of the family of origin. It is qualitatively different; the family of origin has nothing like it. The peer structure is not like a sibling structure; there is no rank assigned by age. One of its vital qualities is that of playfulness; the members can be playful without threatening anyone with too much closeness or loss of face. The members may recognize each other's capacities and assign tasks accordingly. If there is an informal leader, his or her selection may not have occurred without infighting, but the fighting has been among equals. In contrast, perhaps the only time when a genuine peer relationship can emerge in a family is when a husband and wife have succeeded in the remarkable task of creating such a relationship with each other.

We suggest that one of the main reasons why the small, informal group works so well is precisely that its structure does not lend itself to being encumbered by the usual family baggage. Likewise, when an individual is engaged in solo creative or productive work, there is no need to plug into a family system or facsimile thereof.

Focus on the present. The peer group process, or the work of the individual, takes place on the horizontal dimension, the here and now. In contrast, the "ladder" of which Levinson speaks has to do exclusively with the vertical dimension. Efforts and accomplishments on one dimension are rewarded by recognition and progress on the other. The doing may increase skill and capacity, and may result in a climb up the ladder, but doing and climbing should not be confused with each other; for many people at work, climbing means giving up doing what they are invested in doing, whether it is in research, production, sales, or accounting, in order to move up to managerial functions whose perks may never make up for the loss of the intrinsically rewarding activity. The tension between the intrinsic rewards of the here and now and the pull of the vertical structure may be, as we have suggested, very similar to the original tension between the interests of the individual and the pull of the family.

Conflict of interest among peers. We would, of course, be romanticizing if we maintained that the presence of the hierarchical structure was all that stood in the way of people's entering the zone of spontaneity. There is the irreducible reality of people's rivalries with one another. Within academic faculties as well as business organizations, one hears of the "infanticide of ideas." And not all ideas may bestow equal benefits. What the engineering department regards as a brilliant breakthrough may prove to be a source of grief to manufacturing and sales. These things being true, it can make a difference within an organization whether management functions in such a way as to exacerbate the ri-

valries or to encourage an atmosphere of open give-and-take. Negative reinforcement—the withholding of resources, support, and
recognition—a style favored by some managers, is far more likely
to cultivate the rivalry, as is the playing off of subordinates against
one another.

The Facilitators

The view down versus the view across. If people bring family patterns to work with them, what is to prevent them from acting
out these patterns when they reach managerial positions? As
nearly as we have been able to ascertain, the answer is, not much.
In the 1940s, the human relations research staff at the Harvard
Business School, including Elton Mayo, Fritz Roethlisberger,
and George Lombard, developed an advanced concept of what
it meant to be an aware manager, that is, aware of the effects of
his or her own behavior on employees and ready to use this as
a reference point for understanding their reactions. This concept
had much in common with the present-day notion of a person
sufficiently individuated to be able to comprehend his or her part
in relationships. It is hardly necessary to mention that this idea
of management did not catch on. Instead, as Drucker (1974)
observes, the focus in recent decades has tended to be on ''control through psychological manipulation.''

Inherent in this approach is the assumption that the manager
somehow stands outside of and above what is going on with the
employees, moving them about like pieces on a chessboard. This
approach stands in marked contrast to the idea of a process in
which manager and employees are in a state of continual interaction. The manipulative approach totally bypasses the question
of what baggage the manager brings with him. Our observations
and the reports of our clients suggest that there are a lot of
managers out there who are utterly unaware of the impact of how
they act on what gets done. In the American industrial scene,
it is apparently still open season for managers to act however they
choose, which means the door is wide open for family patterns
to exert their effects.

The reality of mistrust. We have already spoken of the importance of trust in maintaining the functioning of small informal work groups. One of the most pernicious family patterns that can intrude into the workplace involves the breakdown of reciprocal trust. Drucker (1974) describes the history of a controversy among industrial psychologists and others about whether people can be trusted to take the initiative at work or whether they will fail to produce unless driven. From our point of view, the argument about what motivates workers, while it does not tell us very much about workers, tells us a lot about how the people on each side of the argument perceive things. As we will spell out in more detail in Chapter 8, the interactions between parents and child during the first few years of life set the tone for the child's later expectations of trust or mistrust. The child may get used to trusting and being trusted, or it may get used to an atmosphere of reciprocal mistrust, and its expectations about trust will determine the quality of all future relationships. An individual bringing the expectation of reciprocal trust into his or her career will probably gravitate toward people with a like attitude; and he or she will probably give out cues that invite reciprocal trusting behavior. Such a person, in spite of occasional encounters with the barracuda of the workplace, will probably find it congenial to think of others as capable of being trusted to function responsibly. In contrast, the person who comes to work steeped in the reciprocities of mistrust may gravitate toward people of like attitude, e.g., the hardheaded union bargainer who can only function when he is up against a ruthless employer. And we can be absolutely certain that this individual will give off showers of cues that invite reciprocal mistrusting behavior. This person will go through life accumulating hard evidence that other people cannot be trusted.

Of course, people's attitudes toward trust are not determined exclusively by their family patterns. Unless engaging in extreme denial, everyone has some ambivalence about how much trust he or she can expect to share with others, if only because there is always some residue from the time in infancy before a sense of trust was established. Anxieties about what is going on at work can reach such a pitch that this latent residue of mistrust gets mobilized. There can be, in other words, a contagion effect, operating semi-independently of the level of trust that people brought with them from home. We have described how the climate of emotionality in a company may be such that destructive attitudes can be transmitted very rapidly downwards from the top office. Mistrust is one of these attitudes.

The supervisor who approaches his or her work force with an attitude of learned mistrust will find it easy to pick up any cues put out by management that the workers are not to be trusted. This supervisor may have very little regard for his or her people as individuals, believing instead that they must be directed like sheep to perform their assigned tasks with certain rewards or punishments to goad them on. His or her constant checking on the work reduces everyone's "discretionary responsibility," a phrase borrowed from McLean (1979). This supervisor can be said to be oriented exclusively on the vertical dimension, relying on authority as a substitute for trust.

At the other end of the spectrum is the supervisor who is aware that unless people are mismatched with their work, most will be able to enter into a dialogue with their job and to become specialists in its performance. What they will need then is not direction so much as support and facilitation. This supervisor is aware that how he or she acts will have a profound effect on whether people are able to mobilize their own efforts or not. Being the boss may mean giving directions, setting and enforcing performance standards, being available to help until it is time to step back, offering encouragement either to stick with a task or to bag it and move on—but always with the recognition that the worker has the potential to emerge as an expert in whatever he or she is doing. This supervisor can be said to be operating on the horizontal dimension, essentially regarding the workers as fellow employees rather than as lower beings. As Wetzel put it (1984), space can be made for a "sideways decision-making process." For the supervisor to be able to adopt such an outlook means being no longer tightly identified with the vertical structure; to achieve this, it seems to us, he or she must have gone through a process of individuation, in relation to both the work and family systems. We do not conceive of this kind of supervisor as a "parent"; one cannot really be a mother or father on company time, and the effort, conscious or unconscious, to become enmeshed in such parental roles can only trigger the very kinds of patterned responses that stand in the way of autonomy. To this supervisor—and to us this is by no means a hypothetical definition of a supervisor, because we have seen it lived out and can attest to its positive impact on productivity—we attach the label of "the facilitator." The person capable of being a facilitator may be invaluable to an organization even while the role he or she plays goes largely unrecognized.

Of course, productive units can quickly become irrelevant if they do not receive directions about what to do or initial directions about how to do it. From this point on, however, the emphasis can start to shift to having the supervisor function as facilitator. Our image about the corporation as a stage production is not a very serious one, but it does have a point. The CEO is positioned, not as an authority on high, but as one who is in a position to facilitate what is going on. The question of how the "boss" can function in this capacity has received a good deal of attention. In contrast to the use of the term "mentor" in corporate politics to refer to the selection and grooming of a protégé and heir, Levinson (1978) speaks of a very special kind of relationship. The mentor functions as teacher, sponsor, host, guide, exemplar. But the mentor, in Levinson's sense, is not a person seeking, overtly or covertly, to set up a parental relationship. The ultimate goal, though it may never be fully realized, is a *peer* relationship.

The boss as a buffer against stress. In ordinary circumstances, the boss can function as a facilitator by acting as a buffer against stress from above. As McLean (1979) points out, the first requirement is that the boss *be there*, his or her very presence providing a kind of reassurance that is far beyond logic. For this kind of presence, the metaphors of "hands-on management" and "management by walking around" are currently in use. As Shakespeare said of King Henry moving among his men as they waited at Agincourt for dawn and battle, the men beheld "a little touch of Harry in the night."

The facilitator makes sure there are tools available to solve problems, conveys confidence that the problems can be solved, and then steps back, moving in again if necessary to give permission to defer a problem or to scrap what has been done and look for a new approach. The work of the facilitator may have to clash with the work of the individual who is trying to define for him- or herself how best to be productive, but each is aware of the need to take the other's position into account. The position of the facilitator is, "the buck stops here," meaning the buck that moves *downwards;* in other words, the facilitator copes with the stresses coming down from higher management, rather than letting these stresses get triangled through into the workplace.

Resistance

The value of autonomy for groups and individuals in organizations has been well documented, yet there has been no rush by business to restructure around this concept. Wetzel (1984) speculates that employers do not know how, that they are skeptical, or that they are afraid of costs and capital risks. To this list of specific factors we can add fear of loss of control. But it seems to us that when we look at business organizations in systemic terms, we begin to see more about why change is slow in coming.

Emotionality. We have already described how sensitive the organizaton is to factors that can generate emotionality. These include factors that have their most immediate effect on top management, such as changes in the economy or in the market. They may include personal factors in the lives of significant people in the organization, such as illness or death of a family member or alcoholism. They also include, of course, the whole range of emotions that can penetrate an organization via the "family baggage"that is brought to work, i.e., the old patterns of response and the emotions associated with them.

The effects of uncertainty. Possibly most significant of all these factors is the sense of uncertainty that must permeate a business organization. Layoffs and firings are always possible, whether through the failure of the individual or through a change in the company. For whatever reason these events may occur, they are never entirely without a sense of stigma and they do not often occur without devastating effect. The way they are handled frequently exacerbates the effect. Arbitrary power to dismiss people on the spot is often put in the hands of individuals who have done nothing to demonstrate that they can or will handle this power responsibly. It may give somebody a thrill indeed to deliver the order: "Clear out your desk by five o'clock!" but we find it hard to imagine that the drama, or the need, can often justify the shock effects on the organization, the disruption of employees' trust in the fairness and good sense of management.

Almost as deep as the fear of dismissal, for many people, and for some people even deeper, goes the fear of being passed over, which may cause lasting devastation to self-esteem.

LaBier (1984) suggests how top appointees in government bureaucracies may seek to short-circuit delay by filling the managerial positions beneath them with "jungle fighters" whose primary credentials are that they know how to "kick ass," using such pressure tactics as humiliation to get quick results. Whatever the short-term payoff, the long-range effect is predictable: greater effort to cover that which has just been kicked. Such self-protective responses only aggravate the bureaucratic inertia.

It is impossible to overemphasize the effects of events such as these that heighten employees' uncertainties. Freud and others have associated depression with fear of loss, a fear that is at the core of most disturbed behavior in families. It may be fear of death in one family, or fear of separation in another, or it can be the more pervasive fear of the loss of self-esteem.

Defensive operations. In response, families mobilize all kinds of defensive operations that are usually debilitating to the family's progress and that of its individual members. Such defenses can include enmeshment, i.e., becoming so entangled in the emotional bonds of the family that there is little remaining sense of self; or rigidity, i.e., functioning according to rules with such inflexible conviction that change cannot occur, as if this could prevent loss from taking place. Both of these defenses can be accompanied by unclear communication, as if change and loss cannot occur as long as nobody has to face anything. Of course, not all families rely on these patterns to the same degree, but the greater the stress, the greater the likelihood that such patterns will begin to emerge.

These patterns of adhering to enmeshment, rigidity, and confusion in order to block change can be carried over very readily into work organizations; indeed, we believe they go a long way to account for what happens in bureaucracies. When anxiety builds up in organizations, people fall back on these defensive patterns because basic instinct says thay have survival value, and basic instinct very often has more clout than logic does. Loyalty gets focused on the preservation of the pattern rather than upon the productive needs of the enterprise.

As far as we know, issues concerning loss have not been faced in industry. Unions have cut down on the incidence of arbitrary layoffs and attempts have even been made to legislate full employment, but the emotional aspects of the issue of loss do not get addressed. Management's expectation of loyalty from employees is stated unilaterally, with no consideration of the fact that the loyalty cannot be reciprocal. The emotional issues stirred up by layoffs are handled by outplacement services where the emphasis is on the *out*; that is, the counseling of laid-off employees is done on the outside by outsiders, and even the outplacement counselors are firmly cautioned to keep the emotions under wraps.

Antidotes to defensive operations. Situations must exist where give-and-take between management and employees is sufficiently open so that there can be realistic expectations on both sides, so that employee commitment and participation can be encouraged in ventures that everyone knows are not going to last forever. To us, this kind of honesty about who can expect what is at the core of "human resources management." Given realistic expectations, employees can be helped to plan their futures, whether inside or outside the company, with enough confidence so the need to cling to outworn defensive patterns is considerably reduced. Of course this kind of management-employee dialogue requires commitment of effort, and some managements may feel that it is more effective to keep their employees off-balance and guessing. But making the effort at open dialogue is the only way that management can make a claim of loyalty *toward* its employees. We believe, in fact, that in the long run good employee relations can mean only relationships of reciprocal awareness and trust. Given this base, the repertoire of methods used as part of human resources management can be effective, whether the issue is one of incentive compensation or Friday afternoon beer busts. But without any base in reciprocal awareness and trust, human resources management methods may, at best, be only as effective as applying a poultice for a broken leg, or, at worst, become counterproductive, and a total sham.

In this chapter, we have outlined some of the ways in which family patterns impact work and exert an influence on the actual processes of work systems in ways that are not in conformance with logic, may not enhance productivity, and have profound implications for the fate of the individual. It is clear, of course, that people do not leave their family baggage at the shop or office door, any more than they can deny their being men and women. And so it appears that further attention to these phenomena will be profitable for corporate managers and human resource personnel as well as for therapists and career counselors.

6

The Effects of the Business
Organization on the Family

Having explored how family systems can affect business organizations, we will focus now on ways that business organizations can affect families.

In certain major respects, what people find at work to take
home with them is positive. As we have mentioned before, work
is the peg most of us hang our identities on, and the position of
the worker helps to give the family a cohesive sense of identity
as well as to establish its place in society. Furthermore, regardless
of its stresses and frustrations, the discipline and the challenge
of work help many people to maintain a reasonably healthy level
of functioning, at least in the work-related area of their lives. This
helps to explain why abrupt retirement can have devastating effects on the physical and mental health of the worker.

The reader will have discovered in this book a systematic bias
toward illustrative material that refers to large corporations. This
is partly due to a bias in our sample; i.e., our experience and the
experience of the majority of our clients has been mostly with
large corporations. Also, the large corporate structure lends itself

better to the kind of conceptualizing we have done so far, because the influences from the family can be more readily sorted out from the influences that are intrinsic to the workplace itself. However, as we consider the interaction between business and family, it is necessary to note that most jobs in this country are still in small businesses, not in the stereotypic Fortune 500 organizations.

In these small businesses, particularly those that are family owned, the boundaries between the personal and the professional are fuzzy at best, and in some instances nonexistent. A person who works in a four-person office may discover that the response of the owner's wife (or husband) to her dress or his necktie is as important as job performance. We know of one company, for example, in which it became impossible for the number-two man to have someone, anyone, over to his house for dinner without offending the boss. The overlap of family and business is so extensive in many cases, and so many unpredictable and often bizarre effects occur, that whoever seeks to function as a consultant or therapist, for the benefit of either the business or the family, is dealing with a deck filled with wild cards, and the only cues as to the values of the cards come from looking at *both* systems and their interactions.

INTERLOCKING TRIANGLES

How They Interlock

In Chapter 4, we described how easy it is to carry patterns from the family to the workplace. In some cases, this means that people at work are unconsciously selected to play the parts of other family members. It may mean that a triangle is set up that includes the worker, a family member, and another member of the work force, e.g., a married couple and the boss, or subordinate, of one of them. Such a triangle opens a conduit for the direct transmission of stress from family to work; e.g., the wife is jealous because her husband pays so much attention to his boss or to his secretary or because he selects a person to be his subor-

dinate of whom the wife disapproves. The same triangular structure can, of course, work the other way around; i.e., the boss
or the secretary, or sometimes even a junior employee, may exert stresses on the worker that flow through to his or her spouse.

In a situation that is only slightly more complicated, Spouse
A may exert pressure on Spouse B, who lets it fall on somebody
at work. Consequently this person, Spouse C, carries it home
to Spouse D, all within a matter of hours.

Thus, the force of legacy, for instance, by means of the mul-
tiplier effect, can make itself felt not only throughout one family, but also throughout an organization of which one member
of that family is a significant member, and thereby throughout
all the families connected with that organization.

Coalitions

When three people are involved in a triangular relationship,
one way to maintain at least a transient equilibrium is for two
of them to form a coalition against the third. It is easy to see how
this can occur within the family or the business structure; it is
just as easy to see how it can occur on the interfaces of work and
family. As we have noted, a spouse may put pressure on his or
her partner to go to work and do something about another employee. This could mean demanding a raise, firing somebody,
being very careful never to have lunch with somebody or meet
somebody by the water cooler.

Or the coalition can be two at work against one at home.
Although the culture seems to be changing gradually, the com-
panies are surely still in the majority in which the expectation
lives on that management-level employees will keep their wives
in line on anything and everything that affects their work. One
executive told us that he could easily imagine his superiors saying, "We don't want him here if he can't control his wife."
Another one said, "The thing I am most afraid of is that someone
will say I am 'pussy-whipped.'" To the degree that supervisors
play into this expectation, the result is to set up a coalition against
the wife, who may in some cases have to live for years with its

effects. In the case of a conflicted marriage, it is of course tempting for one spouse to use others at work for transient or lasting coalitions against the other spouse. This could include events like stopping off for a drink with someone on the way home from work or making arrangements to travel with someone to a convention. (Ironically, these are the same kinds of events that enable people, regardless of their sex, to develop more productive working relationships.) The interpretation of the event by the worker's spouse may or may not be accurate, but even the appearance of a coalition can be enough to cause trouble at home. In the case of Mark (Chapter 1) we saw how a worker-boss-against-wife coalition was replaced by a worker-wife-against-boss coalition.

In those cases where one spouse begins an affair with someone else at work, it is an open question for the clinician whether the affair has any intrinsic merit or whether it serves the aim of an antispouse coalition. As an initial working hypothesis, the notion of coalition usually serves very well, the existence of the coalition being symptomatic of marital difficulty. In this kind of situation, of course, the exchange of stresses between work and home can become riotous.

The "Revolving Slate"

Boszormenyi-Nagy (Boszormenyi-Nagy & Spark, 1973) has introduced this term to refer to what is almost certainly the most pernicious effect of triangular relationships. In a situation where loyalty, particularly loyalty to a parent, prevents one individual from retaliating directly against another for abuse of any kind, the victimized individual may select a substitute object upon whom to direct the retaliation. Such abuse may go ricocheting down through generations within a family, and its effects may spread outside the family. If the abuser has been a parent, the victim may be spouse, child, or employee. A man whose father was sadistic may behave in a similar way toward his employees. The employee, in turn, rather than making retaliatory moves toward the employer, may take the animus home and direct it, depending on his or her own past patterning, against spouse,

child, or even against the teachers at a school board meeting
when the opportunity arises. Thus, through the process of the
"revolving slate," unconscious hostility of quite specific origins
may lead to very active targeting of people on the other side of
the home-work boundary. When it occurs, this process serves
as a substantial reinforcer of whatever other hostile moves are
occurring in home-work triangles.

Negative Entitlement

Suppose as a clinician one is dealing with the common situation in which the wife complains that the husband is coming
home utterly drained by his work and uses the family like a "pit
stop," with no regard for anyone's needs except his own. She
may, for instance, bitterly resent his strewing the papers from
his briefcase about the sun porch on weekends, a gin and tonic
in hand and the stereo holding the family at bay, while their 10-
year-old daughter wanders the neighborhood honing her skills
as a kleptomaniac. But the husband may stonewall any confrontation on this issue and feel quite justified in his actions. His conscious justification might be something like, "You owe me this
so that I can go back out on Monday to earn money for you."
His unconscious formulation may run like this: "It is being taken
away from me at work, I am entitled to take it away from you
at home, and where you go to get it back is your business, not
mine." This may be an echo from his past, when his father
similarly victimized the family. Of course, his subjective sense of
justice is not in accord with the realities, but it does not lose any
of its potency because of that. Indeed, he may be unconsciously or quite consciously pursuing what he regards as his own survival, fearing that if he allows himself to become vulnerable to
the domestic stresses his wife is seeking to impose on him, these
might so aggravate the stress from work that he could appear
weak to his work associates, or he could even suffer such a dire
effect as a heart attack. Thus, the sense of "negative entitlement"
may support one spouse in preserving what is essentially a grossly unbalanced triangle, the workplace continuing to be the bene-

ficiary of what is drained from the family. This can go on indefinitely unless the husband begins to reexamine the nature of his relationship to his employer. Of course, a situation like a kleptomaniac daughter is not so frequently encountered; what is more likely to emerge is a lament that the husband sees no reason why he should have to engage in ordinary activities, such as putting up a window box or going to a museum.

WHAT THE WORKPLACE EXPECTS OF THE HOME

In what has become the traditional set of expectations of corporate employees, the structure of the home is supposed to dovetail with the structure at work. As at work, the functions of the two spouses are to be carefully differentiated. The wife is to be responsible for the domestic duties. The husband may "help out" with the dishes or even the laundry, as long as it is clearly defined that this is *her* work he is helping out with. The husband will spend some time with the children each night, if time permits, as well as certain blocks of time with the family on weekends, although this can occasionally become problematic if golf with colleagues or customers interferes. The husband is expected to deal with "handyman" chores about the house, but if he is inept or disinterested the wife after years of frustration may have taken over the toolbox. As for big items like household furnishings, major repairs, or additions to the house, the husband often expects to have the last word, so that expenses can be kept under control, but he may not be available very often to say what the last word is. She may or may not know how much money they have, if any. He may or may not go to P.T.A. meetings. If a child gets out of line, the husband is expected to take firm action, even if this is of the paratrooper variety, quick-in and quick-out again.

The husband may bring home his troubles from work and the wife will be a listener, but it is usually considered to be better form if he keeps matters concerning work to himself. If she has a problem and wants to talk about it, he may have a solution framed and ready to deliver almost before she is finished. If, as is quite possible, her purpose in talking was not to borrow a solution but to work out one of her own, she may react to his solution with annoyance, and her annoyance may leave him bewildered, perhaps muttering, as he leaves the scene, "Well, what more can I tell you?"

In this kind of traditional alignment, the husband may be quite explicit in his belief that somebody has to be the chief. Of course, depending on how things are at work, this may be the only chance the husband gets to play chief. In some cases, the husband may attempt to carry the dovetailing of work and home to its logical extreme; i.e., the home is run as an *extension* of work, as if family members were employees, with rules laid down, orders given, jobs delegated, no back talk permitted—an approach that sooner or later is likely to have explosive consequences because it does not take into account the realities of family process.

This differentiated family structure, the husband working and the wife taking care of the home, is often referred to as "teamwork," and there are many couples for whom this concept is still genuinely applicable. We must acknowledge that this division of labor was traditionally regarded as fair. On the other hand, for women who are interested in working, the concept that part of the team can never get onto the playing field is hard to grasp, and this has contributed to a rethinking of what is fair.

The traditional kind of family structure is regarded as one that will operate with less friction, that is, less *overt* friction, than the home in which there is a messy overlap between the husband's functions and the wife's. The differentiation of function means in most cases that the husband does not learn the practical and emotional skills required of anyone who is going to be a full-scale parent. It appears that men are far more likely than women to be shattered by the sudden realization that, due to the spouse's sudden departure or death, they must abruptly assume the whole burden of the children. This is true even if the woman who must assume this burden is already carrying a full-time job. The differentiation of function also plays into the postdivorce phenomenon of the "weekend father," whose contribution to the children's welfare consists of taking them to the zoo, and who lets meaningful daily contact with his children go by default. The popularity of such father-son activity programs as "Indian Guides" does something to fill what otherwise might be a vacuum in the father-son relationship, but at best it is a substitute for the father's meaningful participation in the son's life. Divorce lawyers, preparing their male clients to ask for joint custody, sometimes have to coach them on how to make a school visit.

Since this kind of family structure is organized around the husband's working life, attention to which so often gets priority over other interests, the family may be rendered quite vulnerable to any and all stresses coming from that quarter. Late work and working weekends are, of course, a common source of friction, and it is not unheard of for families to have to organize their lives around the schedule of a bachelor boss who would rather get back to his apartment later than sooner. Transfers can, of course, be traumatic; we know of one executive wife who flatly refused to hang the same curtains for the nineteenth time. Having the life of the family thus directed from some unseen source can give the wife a deep sense of being powerless, equivalent to being held hostage.

What may be a source of pleasure for some wives is a bitter pill for others who are expected to show deferential behavior toward their husband's bosses and their wives on social occasions. We know of one woman who seriously considered meeting her husband and his boss at the door dressed liked a domestic servant.

While the patterns described above are still the prevailing ones for perhaps a majority of single-career families, we have encountered very few couples in recent years in which the nonworking member has not become openly dissatisfied with the basic premises of this kind of marriage. The wife may complain that to her husband the job is a "mistress." She may complain that he puts her "second" behind the job, or "third" behind the job and the children, or maybe "fourth" behind the job, the children, and the sailboat. In looking at it this way she may be ranking everything along a single dimension, i.e., the amount of time he spends with each. Possibly she is overlooking qualitative differences in the husband's emotional response to different parts of his life. Or her complaint may turn out to be wholly legitimate; even so, the cumulative impact of her complaints may have deadened the husband's capacity to respond to them. This is the usual result of a wife's active assault on the habits of a workaholic husband. The wife who used to limit her response to ''bitching and moaning'' about her husband's workaholism is much more likely now to be engaged in an active counterstrategy such as developing new interests, exploring career options, looking at what divorce might bring, entering therapy to look at her own part in the marital impasse, or any combination of the above.

The man's complaint may be just as bitter about the failure of the working wife to provide care and meet emotional needs. Both feel that they are being robbed of something to which they are absolutely entitled. As one executive whose wife's litany had to do with his indifference, put it, ''No matter which way I turn I'm cheating somebody. I want to handle my people at work gently, but that takes time and I can't make the time. I don't know how much longer I can go on letting my work slide.'' In this tight triangle that embraces the workplace and the family, stress at any point can be immediately conveyed to the other points, with multiplying effects.

THE COUNTERTREND

The contemporary counterpressure being exerted by wives makes for significant alterations in family structure. The male may enter gladly into greater participation at home or he may be dragged by the heels, kicking and screaming all the way, and the ensuing turbulence may seem as if it were going to wreck the family, although we have not yet met a couple who were about to divorce because of the conflict that arose when the working spouse *did* get more involved in the family.

With the breakdown of the neatly differentiated family structure, there is an emerging need for more effective *negotiation* between spouses, and from our point of view negotiation is by no means synonymous with the term *communication*, as it is used often to refer to the process of expressing one's thoughts and emotions to someone else. Negotiation requires a particular kind of discipline, which will be described at length in Chapter 10. The active, ongoing balancing of work and family as well as self-interests is a process that never occurs without some friction, yet it can yield the most enriching results. Perhaps the "state of the art" marriage for the foreseeable future is one that can survive because competition between the spontaneously emerging interests of husband and wife can be successfully negotiated.

In the case of George, we explore some of the impact of the corporation on the family. Like that of Roberta in Chapter 2, this is a composite case.

THE CASE OF GEORGE

George was an executive with fast-track aspirations. It was important to him what style briefcase he carried and what brand of shirt, suit, tie, and shoes he wore, for he believed that these symbols helped convey his readiness to move up the ladder. His wife, Susan, by her own account, "bitched and moaned" because he put his work first, his children second, and her third, but he insisted that he was only doing what he had to do to "make it."

George usually got home about 7:30 P.M. and began almost at once to prepare for his 6 A.M. rising. He stayed late at the office some nights, brought work home with him on weekends, and took frequent trips out of town. Susan objected to his hours. As far as she was concerned, she was a single parent. He argued that he was never away from home more than two nights at a time. She told him that "getting back at midnight doesn't count."

Their son, Becket, was in second grade, and one reason Susan had pushed for treatment was that the teacher had called Becket a very anxious child. He did good work but panicked over errors and he was terrified by the fire alarm.

Susan blamed her son's vulnerability on lack of fathering, but George complained bitterly that everything would have been all right if Susan had only taken charge of things at home. She babied Becket, he said, and she let their 14-year-old daughter,

Ellen, get away with murder. Beyond that, he added, she left the house a mess and did not entertain properly. It seemed to George that his wife just could not keep up.

In the first full family session, it became evident soon enough that the mother and the two children formed a coalition against the father. Susan presented Becket's school problem to support the charge that George had neglected his son. In defense, George confronted Becket: "Do I neglect you? Don't I read to you at night?" Caught in the split between his parents, Becket's reply was to start crying, which prompted George to snap at his wife: "Can't you see how you've babied him?" And, reacting to this attack on mother, Ellen said tearfully, "But, Dad, what Mother said was true. You don't ever listen to me. You never show any feelings for me."

This final confrontation seemed to reach George, who sat motionless and gazed in stony silence at a point on the far wall.

The therapist intervened: "Can you respond to your daughter?"

"When I think her feelings are genuine, I'll respond to her."

"George, it must be very lonely over there, the therapist said."

It took weeks before the therapist could begin to get an adequate sense of the family. George's father had died early; George had been supported, and his private schooling had been paid for by his father's two sisters, who had made it clear to George's mother that they expected results from George; he was to accomplish all that his father had not. George's mother, now 70, was in failing health and "lived for" word of her son's successes. He quite concretely believed that by feeding her good news he was keeping her alive. And good news, of course, meant promotions, bonuses, stock options, and rides in the company jet.

But George felt inward dread that his career was not going right. At 38 his future in the company was uncertain. His superior seemed aloof and gave nothing but peremptory orders and criticism of the results. This was, indeed, the style of the company. What George dreaded most was any hint that his colleagues would see him as a man who took direction from his wife. On the surface, he was furious at Susan for failing to perform the magic of the corporate wife, taking charge at home, and entertaining on cue. He resented her for failing to stand shoulder-to-shoulder with him as a team dedicated to his success. Below the surface, George was projecting onto Susan and the children all his own never-expressed fear of being inept.

This covert aspect of George's attitude turned out to be the most critical aspect that had shaped Susan's response. The continual sense of having her role derogated had, over the years, made it impossible for her to take effective command of events at home.

George had been enmeshed not only with his mother but also with the family designation that was an imperative mandate to succeed. He had not completed what McGoldrick and Carter (1982) call the *second-order* change of separating from his parents and formulating his own goals, which might even have involved a reassessment of his choice of or his approach to work. But until the work of separation was done, or at least the need for it acknowledged, there would not be much prospect of his coping effectively with his family. His ability to eventually share his fear in joint sessions with Susan was a major movement not only toward individuation but also toward saving the relationship. And unless the therapist had guided the couple toward the career aspect of the problem, this movement might never have occurred.

7

Cross Traffic

In the preceding chapters our focus has been on the family as a significant variable intervening between the individual and his or her work. We have examined this theme from three perspectives: the effect of the family on what the individual does at work, the effect of the family on the work organization in which the individual functions, and the countereffects of the work organization on the family. In this chapter we will explore some of the background factors that have a special impact on the interactions among the family, the individual, and work. These background factors deal with the meshing of individual and family life cycles and the points of conflict that arise when the cycles fail to synchronize.

THE TIMING OF CAREER CHOICE

For many people the issue of career choice presents a special irony. At least in our culture, as McGoldrick and Carter (1982) point out, going to work provides critical leverage for the process of individuation. We assume that the process of individuation will be well under way by late adolescence and that normal young people will be able to "stand on their own feet" by their early to mid-twenties. By this time, they are likely to have finished college, an event that symbolizes separation from the family. So for people who are still in their early 20s, the pressure to take on that all-important pivotal job has become compelling, unless they undertake additional years in graduate school in order to increase the odds of a secure future.

Meanwhile, the family is often in the position of having invested many thousands of dollars in a college education for a son or daughter who appears to be at a loss for what to do with his or her life, all this at a time when the benefits of such an investment are coming under increasing scrutiny in our society. The parents, therefore, are likely to be looking almost desperately for some relief from the cash outflow as well as for some kind of return on their investment, if only in the form of some evidence that their sacrifice might pay off. Even if the son or daughter goes to work instead of attending college, the gap between his or her living expenses and initial earnings may still impose a financial burden on the family. To many parents, whose own narcissism is at stake in their son's or daughter's career choice, getting a return on their investment means seeing the offspring ensconced in a "real job" that will provide some clear answers about what the financial and social status of the child is going to be.

And while this is going on, the young person, even if he or she has just finished a program with a career-related major such as administration or communications, may not have found any opportunity to get beyond the most superficial assessment of his or her own capacities and interests. And there may not appear to be any tools at hand for doing so.

Faced with this dilemma, some young adults look for alternatives by taking a year off to travel or to work for a volunteer agency, hoping the experience will improve their awareness of themselves, their values, and their career inclinations. This can be a wise delaying action, although parents may fear that their offspring will never get back on track.

It is more likely, of course, that the young person will choose to enter a job, doing so in a state of considerable uncertainty or even trepidation, searching among the ambiguous clues for signs of how well the job and the self are going to fit. Staying in a job may prove costly if the best fit available is an uneasy compromise that gradually narrows and warps the self until the retrospections of middle age bring a sense of defeat and bitterness. Leaving, however, may be quite costly in terms of the threat to self-esteem and the turmoil aroused in significant others such as family, friends, and spouse.

For a person confronted with such a dilemma, the late 20s, as Levinson (1978) has pointed out, can be an unsettling and turbulent period. This outcome can often be attributed to an ironic accident of timing; i.e., the process of individuation may require commitment to work long before the person is ready through training or experience to make a good choice of work.

What sometimes happens then is what one might suspect would happen: burdened by the initial, superficial career choice, the person does not continue to move toward individuation; instead, the apparent surface movement merely conceals a transfer of dependencies from the biological parents to the surrogate parents of the workplace. Old patterns may thus get transferred intact, without the opportunity for revision in the light of self-awareness.

A later event may force the individual to face what has occurred. Take, for example, a 30-year-old who came to treatment because his girlfriend's pressure for a commitment had thrown him into a panic. It turned out that he had unconsciously put his life on hold because of ambivalence about his initial career choice. He needed to rework that choice before life closed in on him, and until he did so he would be unable to make any commitments. However, if nothing like this occurs to disrupt the prolongation of the old dependent patterns, they will affect the growth of both the individual and the company in which he or she is placed.

Even for those who are truly engaged in learning how they and the working world are going to fit together, early adulthood can be a lonely and uncertain period, when the only identifying data that turn up with any clarity may be the labels on one's jeans. But given the profusion of career options available for those who are driven by their designations to achieve, no young adult has to settle for grabbing the brass ring the first time around. We can afford the delay required either to defer or to reexamine initial career choices. We are also on the way to developing the kinds of resources that will help young adults to make their initial career choice an informed one.

ABOUT THE CONTINUATION OF CAREER CHOICE

In the second decade of one's working life the individual may be struck by a second irony. The first time around, the pressure on the person to continue his or her personal growth could easily result in a poorly informed career choice, with later detrimental effects upon one's personal as well as working life. This time the person may be confronted with the irony of accepting promotion in order to continue the pursuit of his or her life goals, without being ready to make an informed decision about whether or not to *give up* the mastery aquired in one's former position, so as to move to "higher" levels of the organization, levels that may turn out eventually to be arid plateaus. In one case, a person with known expertise in the design of optical equipment accepted a supervisory position only in response to pressure from his peers. As long as he could continue to be out on the floor among his men the department went well, but the job required him to do a substantial amount of paperwork, and when he was engaged in it he felt as if he were wandering in a wasteland. The ranks of middle management may begin to seem increasingly faceless as the direct connection between one's own effort and the output of the company becomes increasingly vague—so vague in fact that a consultant hired to rediscover the connection may not be able to do so. One strong voice somewhere within the person may be calling out, "Keep climbing!" while another voice may be answering back from somewhere else within the person, "Climbing *what?*"

In both instances described above in which a decision about careers must be made, the first occurring in the early to late 20s, the second occurring in the early 40s, what appear to be realistic demands upon one's self to "grow up" may in fact undercut what the self intrinsically has to offer.

OTHER BAD FITS

An article in a recent issue of the *Harvard Business School Bulletin* (Day, 1985) is accompanied by an illustration that contains "his" and "hers" Superman capes and attaché cases. The illustration makes the point that a young couple setting out together for a life adventure on the "fast track" are likely to expect, in spite of everything they have learned to the contrary, that the fast track is truly an express lane with no cross traffic. In fact, the kinds of interruptions and detours that the couple are likely to encounter probably will be more like the road conditions of the 1920s. Our society gives us no reason to take for granted a preexisting goodness of fit between the requirements of our lives as individuals, family members, and members of the working world. What coordination we do achieve usually comes as the result of stressful effort. The husband who recently asked one of us in a state of genuine perplexity, "But *why* can't two people live together as smoothly as one?" was perhaps being guided by some fantasy of time that never was. There are a number of potential conflict points, a few of which are discussed below.

Crosscurrents of Changing Expectations

It has become virtually axiomatic that a couple entering into the first few years of marriage will have to go through an often turbulent period of adjustment regarding their unconscious expectations of each other. The shapes such expectations can take are by now well known: the spouse can take the place of the parent, the spouse can provide the pieces necessary to complement the self, or the spouse can provide an ambience of warmth and intimacy without slipping any burrs under the pillow. The self-image may take a severe beating as it gradually becomes apparent that what is actually happening in the marriage does not fit with what was vaguely expected. Each spouse may struggle either to face or to ward off questions like, "Am I really any good at this?" Meanwhile, a parallel process may be occurring at work, and what happens at work will not wait for the resolution of what happens at home. The hopes concerning what one may become and the fear of becoming a failed self, both rubbing against one's perception of what the employer wants one to be, may throw a person into a state of turbulence.

Simultaneously with the turbulence being stirred up at home and at work due to the dissonance between expectations and realities, the marriage is being stressed from another quarter. Marriage means institutionalization, beginning with the wedding, which in spite of popular myths to the contrary is designed to meet the social needs of the extended families, not just the couple. Especially when the first child is born, this seals a formal connection between two families of origin, with all the structural implications. Now there are grandparents, aunts, and uncles. The new couple is locked in between the grandparents and the children in an intergenerational chain. The focus tends to shift away from the association of two peers; the family-of-origin systems have more opportunity to assert themselves, and the movement toward individuation may endure heavy stress. With one's self-esteem simultaneously "up for grabs" both at home and at work, it is commonplace for frustrations experienced in one area to seek expression in the other, sometimes through the derogation of the spouse or a subordinate. This may occur, of course, just when the spouse or subordinate is equally vulnerable.

Conflicting Realities

A husband's acceptance of the first important promotion at work or his decision to strike out on his own in a new company may bring a rapid escalation of work demands, more or less coinciding with the decision to get a family under way. In the husband's view, he may be doing what is suitable and appropriate if he devotes himself wholeheartedly to the demands of the job. But this course of action may not turn out to work very well. Just

as stubborn as the demands of work on the husband may be the
demands on the wife to cope with the burdens of solitude imposed by pregnancy and infant care. Her realistic claim for his
support may, in the balancing of long-term interests, be as important to the success of their lives as the claims imposed upon
him by his work. Many couples lack either any advance thought
of how they are going to approach these questions of balance or
even any polite vocabulary to put the questions into words. Some
couples are doing what they can to get a jump on the problems
of coordination they are going to face, for example, by timing a
pregnancy to coincide with the slack season of the year for an
accountant/husband.

Timing for the Dual-Career Family

The issues surrounding questions of family planning for dual-
career families are now of course receiving a great deal of attention. Questions of timing may turn on purely personal preferences. Some women, contemplating full commitment to a career,
might not even wish to imagine a scenario in which they would
have to cancel out at work in order to care for a sick child. Some
women might find themselves able to share this burden with a
spouse. The attitude of the employer or the accessibility of day-
care services or of help from other family members might make
a critical difference.

Subtle variations in attitudes toward mothering may also have
relevance to the outcome. A desire to be a "good enough" mother could lead a woman in either direction, toward work or toward
full-time attention to the offspring through early childhood. A
narcissistic investment in being the "ideal" mother, the Super-
woman of motherhood, may fill one with excessive guilt and
regret if one cannot be home for every precious moment of the
child's unfolding. It may be hard to weigh whether the neglect
imposed upon a child by the mother's career would actually be
worse than the neglect imposed by a mother whose vitality ebbed
because she had to stay home. The prospect of reentry into the
job market buoys many women during the child-raising years,

but there may be nagging questions about whether one is going to be able to compete with younger entrants when the time comes. It is not surprising, nor does it seem in the least unnatural, that many women still opt for the traditional pattern of home-making and that for many women this will prove fulfilling.

As with the other issues of timing mentioned above, what we consider to be the most important consideration here is the simple fact that a couple cannot set their course on ''automatic'' if they wish to get the desired results. The coordination of the demands of family and work upon the person is a matter that will for the foreseeable future continue to require the joint attention of husbands and wives, and in this context employers will also be called upon more and more for moves toward solutions.

The Issues Presented by Aging Parents

While increasing attention is given to the practical needs of older persons, there is still a vast *terra incognita* of relationships among adults and their aging parents. This too can create unexpected cross traffic along one's career path. Suppose, for instance, that a man has reached his 40s; he may be getting a little concerned about keeping up with younger men, he may be struggling with the first strong intimations of mortality, he may find that his children are giving him a hard time as they advance into their late teens, he may have doubts about his marriage and uncertainties about his career, yet none of these may cause him the anguish he feels in relation to his own parents.

As the man in question individuated and matured, what emerged to bestow meaning in his life has moved him away from what holds meaning for his parents. His work, place of residence, associations, functioning as a parent and as a spouse, together may constitute a world about which his parents have no understanding and to which they can give no recognition. In order to come alive in their eyes he would have to go back to reoccupy an old, outmoded shell of self. Staying alive on his terms may impose upon him the numbing realization that he will never again be—if he ever was—fully in touch with them no matter how much he struggles to fashion points of contact. To make what we are saying concrete through what is obviously an extreme example, one of us is currently helping a woman to prepare for a visit from her parents who, if their past conduct is a guide, will wander into the neighbor's yard and attempt to divert the neighbor with tales of what a bad little girl their daughter was—to which she will be expected to respond with suitable contriteness. The message they will convey is that, no matter what she has made of her life, it doesn't count, she has never overcome their disapproval. In our experience, the realization by adults that this kind of gap exists between them and their parents can never be casually dismissed; it puts the sense of self-worth to an ultimate test, and it may be accompanied by the deepest kind of anguish, at a time when other uncertainties in one's life are also tugging at whatever convictions one has about one's self and one's work. What we have already observed applies here as well, that in matters of this kind there is no preexisting set of guidelines and that trying to find some point of renewal with parents may be a matter requiring the most carefully considered effort, even though there may never be the dreamed of recognition and reward.

Ironically, while work is a central part of life, people's life cycles do not always mesh in ways that create an easy path for careers.

8

Sources of Tension Over
Performance

Between the individual's efforts to perform and the expectations of other family members toward that individual, a tension can begin building, as early as the first few days of life, that will rarely be absent for the remainder of one's life and that will have an effect, sometimes a profound one, on how one functions in any sort of work setting. In Chapter 2 we began the discussion of this process; now we would like to explore it in greater depth, beginning with factors in infancy and early childhood that have an effect on how the child is going to perform.

INFANCY

The cries and movements of the newborn, as Erikson (1950) and Mahler (1979) have observed, give evidence that the infant can easily reach the threshold of feeling overwhelmed by inner discomforts. Without any conscious volition the infant is hard at work to gain better control of everything that goes on inside. How the parenting figure responds will, of course, make a crucial difference in whether this work proceeds within reasonable bounds of discomfort or whether it becomes permeated with tension.

The ideal is the reliable parenting figure who can balance the gratification of the child's needs with appropriate restraints and delays so that the child will begin to build tolerance for tension. Without such tolerance, the child would never be free enough from immediate sensory stimuli to be able to think or plan. Thus, ideally, a rhythm of gratification and restraint develops between the child and the nurturing figure. When this occurs, then in Mahler's (1979) terms the child will develop a "confident expectation" that this rhythm will be preserved. And the ensuing trust that grows between parent and child during this process becomes the basic template for all the child's later excursions into relational trust. If the rhythm breaks down, if the child is allowed to suffer too long without relief or is smothered with relief too soon, what Erikson (1950) calls "basic trust" may never be firmly established.

Most parents are able to become "good enough" parents to keep the rhythm going, but of course the outcome is never perfect; at best an infant's needs are hard to gauge and parents cannot routinely be at their best. Inevitably, some degree of tension will build between parent and child as the child's need to function, by crying, crawling, running, and clutching, comes into conflict with the parent's sense of correct behavior. This tension is the precursor of later tensions that will arise in connection with issues around how the child achieves and what is defined as achievement.

EARLY CHILDHOOD

By the time the child is able to talk, a whole host of factors begins to impinge on the way he or she performs. Cultural and ethnic expectations of course play a significant part; these may, for instance, designate that girls are not supposed to engage in as much risk taking as boys or that children are not allowed to debate their parents' decisions. Even in a relatively sophisticated suburban household, a nine-year-old girl who states the firm conviction that her entitlement to make decisions is on a par with her parents' is likely to throw the parents off balance so that they are unable to respond.

Other factors exerting a strong influence on the young child's performance include, of course, the legacy and designation factors we described in Chapter 3. A son, for instance, may receive subtle or not so subtle clues from his mother that if he patterns his efforts after his father's he can expect her ridicule, while if he imitates his maternal uncle his mother will be delighted. Interwoven throughout the parents' messages about how the children are to behave are special bulletins designating how this child is to function in this family. An extreme example may be given of two brothers, the youngest and oldest of three boys, whose mother stands behind them while they are wrestling, and gives covert hand signals to the younger one not to be rough with his big brother, whose physical condition is known to be delicate and who, years later, dies. The grown-up youngest brother is assailed by an anxiety attack when offered a new position that will pay a higher salary than the surviving middle brother is making.

Also, as we indicated in Chapter 3 on designation, reality factors can affect the tension between parents and children over issues of performance. The economic condition of the family may determine, for instance, whether the parents have extra time to help the child learn skills, whether tools will be available, whether the child will be expected to give up his or her own interests in order to help out, etc.

A much larger class of reality factors has to do with the child's endowment—intelligence and aptitudes. Simply being bright and inquisitive can, in the extreme case, put a child at a disadvantage in a family where the parents have entered into a mutual-defense pact whereby they denigrate anything that appears as a challenge to their own competence. Or the fact that the child's interests are merely *different* from the parents' can make it hard for the parents to give permission, show interest, or provide support.

Along with differences of interest may come emerging differences of style, and these may be a fertile source for escalation of tension. A mother wants her daughter's school books back in the bag at night so there will be one less fuss in the morning. Her daughter sees the minutes required to pack school books as an infringement on her last few precious moments of stay-up time. When such an issue as this is unraveled it may reveal something about the structure and functioning of the family, but the immediate by-product is an increase in mother-daughter tension that may still be sticking to the pages of the school books when it is time to read.

PARENTAL CONTRIBUTIONS

As we have indicated before, the nature of tension between parents and children may be a reflection of the nature of the parents' own narcissistic needs. These often have to do with wanting the child to serve as caretaker, but parental narcissism can also find expression in the control of the child's performance. There seems to be a very fine line between providing a child with suitable guidance and habitually blunting the thrust of the child's own initiative. The parents may also have specific concerns about how the child is going to function outside the family. The family may, for instance, be one that seeks to protect its image from the ravages of the outside world by maintaining a very low profile. Such a family is described by Sperry, Staver, Reiner, and Ulrich (1954): the father may undercharge his customers, refuse vacations because the boss has not had one, or go to work when he is ill for fear his absence would make too much work for someone else; the mother may devote her efforts to playing the role of placater, giving Christmas gifts to hostile neighbors, accepting visitations from whole families of relatives no matter how untimely, and going without help when ill or in distress. In such a family, the message to the child is that aggressive competition is wrong while self-effacement and self-sacrifice are right.

Or as Sperry et al. observe, one or both parents may have elected one of the child's siblings to serve as the bearer of aggression and the successful rival.

The mother may need to play out her legacy by derogating anything that is distinctly male, which to her may include anything that is distinctly assertive. Through such simple messages as complaining that her son's haircut looks "masculine and tough," she may convey her warnings. If these kinds of messages are pushed often enough and hard enough by the parents, the result can, for example, extend to a serious inhibition of the child's academic performance.

The opposite message, that the parents want the child to achieve so they can gather the vicarious fruits of the child's performance, can also, of course, have an inhibitory effect if it is their dominant message in their life with the child. As noted earlier, this can be especially binding if the child's achievements are expected to make up for those that never came to pass because another sibling died or failed. Or the parent may unconsciously regard the child's successes as absolution from guilt over a congenital birth defect or other shortcoming in the child, while the child's failures may be taken as proof that the parent is to blame.

Boszormenyi-Nagy and Spark (1973) put the question of the child's separation squarely in the context of an ambivalent and conflicted relationship with the parents.

> The child who is able to make a move toward separation must sooner or later face his guilt and the awareness that his parents will experience grief and hidden resentment over his move. Ultimately the process leads to obsolescence of the older generation. *This existential fact must be recognized as the major source of stress in family life.* (italics ours) (p. 153)

Those achievements of the child that are necessary to bring about separation remind the parents of their own movement toward obsolescence. For the child some degree of anxiety over performance is therefore unavoidable, and this anxiety is of a nature that can intrude directly at work. A son who had previously worked as an assistant to his father in the father's company, and who was attempting to take career steps that would get him out of his father's shadow, found himself having anxiety attacks in the middle of meetings with potential customers; for a few moments he would simply become mute. The problem was relieved when its context was understood. The kind of tough "have your desk empty by 5 P.M." style that characterizes some corporate executives may have its roots, quite simply, in the older generation's hostility toward the younger; this style and the hostile attitude underlying it are masquerading as skill in maintaining command.

THE STRUGGLE AMONG SELVES

All of the above factors contribute, of course, to what we described in Chapter 3 as the process of designation. The designated self incorporates the injunctions from ethnic background, culture, socioeconomic factors, family legacies and values, and narcissistic parental needs, as well as the realities of the child's own capacities and spontaneous interests. A conscientious parent might be horrified by this inventory of factors that can affect a child's efforts. Our intent here is not to descend into deeper guilt about parenting, but to look realistically at the motivational factors that the grown child will be carrying with him or her to the workplace, how these affect careers, and how the awareness of this can help towards individuation.

In the normal course of development during early adulthood, a somewhat chaotic struggle may take place. The person may still be having a hard time sorting out what his or her real inclinations are: whether, for example, to stay in a large corporation, seek out a small company, or undertake something on one's own or with a partner; whether to go back to school, move from teaching into business, from marketing into communications, etc. The attempt to arrive at some sense of the actual self must be carried out while the voices of one's designated self are still being loudly heard and while the organization for which one works is dictating its own definition of a desirable employee. At this stage, a person's own doubts about how to resolve these conflicting demands may leave one especially vulnerable to whatever might sound like adverse feedback from others. In all of this, the person is searching for the best fit among what appear to be his or her resources, what appear to be available in the way of opportunities, what he or she dreams of as the fulfillment of the ideal self, and what the family can tolerate. The perceived gap between the most fearful assessment and the most hopeful one can be the source of a great deal of discouragement, leading sometimes to clinical depression.

JOINT DISPLACEMENTS

In the sections above we have already said a good deal about how emotional tensions from one area may be displaced onto another; e.g., a parent's apprehension about obsolescence can alter his or her attitude toward a child's performance. Two or more people can jointly engage in such displacements. In one family, a mother and daughter were locked into an incessant struggle having to do with the daughter's schedule for the afternoon and evening. Returning from private day school about five o'clock, the nine-year-old daughter was expected to fit her homework, piano practice, household chores, etc. into the hours before her nine-thirty bedtime—not an unreasonable expectation. Yet by ten o'clock, regardless of the parents' and older sister's efforts at supervision, the mother would discover her daughter watching television, her homework and other chores untouched. Notes from teachers arrived regularly to reinforce the mother's concern. In the superheated atmosphere, escalation of orders from the mother brought only escalation of angry complaints from her daughter about being ordered around. To this militant nine-year-old, there was not a single valid reason why children should not have the same authority over parents that parents have over children.

In a move to break the deadlock between parent and child, their therapist introduced a visualization exercise in which the daughter was invited to think of their conflict as one occurring between two symbolic objects, such as animals. Before the instructions were finished, the daughter's fingers were curling up to form claws. She announced, "I am a tiger, and mother is a lion."

"What are you doing?" asked the therapist.

"We are fighting."

"What are you fighting about?"

"We are fighting about which one is prettier."

To this girl there were no distinctions between struggling over homework and struggling over any other aspect of life that could be invested with mother-daughter rivalry; school achievement and the goal of thwarting her mother had already become linked. Accustomed to being stripped of privileges such as watching TV and attending birthday parties, the girl explained her misbehavior by saying that when she made trouble for her mother it took away her mother's privileges and made things come out even.

As the mother and daughter described their battles, it became evident that the daughter's sense of deprivation had something to do with the fact that the father had recently felt compelled to terminate his corporate job and had not yet found a suitable alternative, a turn of events that was deeply upsetting to the family. Further exploration revealed that on two or three occasions when the mother and daughter were in the midst of a fierce argument, the daughter had collapsed sobbing into her mother's arms.

In this family, the mother-daughter conflict over schoolwork not only served as a medium of expression for the sexual aspects of mother-daughter rivalry, but also kept the family in balance; the daughter was acting as a lightning rod to divert the force of existing mother-father conflicts, which stemmed in part from the severe obstacles the maternal grandmother had put in the way of this mother's access to her father. The stress resulting from the father's surrender of his job put an overload on the mother-father-daughter triangle; the daughter, in addition to involving her mother in conflict over her schoolwork, was giving voice to the family depression, and thereby pulling the parents together in their concern for her.

Needless to say, the inroads on this child's capacity for achievement would have become increasingly severe if the parents and child had not broken out of their deadlock, a feat they accomplished fairly rapidly because the mother was able to respond to her daughter's openness in the therapeutic sessions. Not long afterwards the girl presented the therapist with three school reports: The first stated that she had made the honor roll for effort. That came as a surprise. The second announced that she had made the honor roll for artistic work. That was not such a surprise because the homework over which she and her mother fought did not include art. The third carried the news that she had made the honor roll for academic achievement.

The theme of rivalry can also be seen in the case of a mother and a daughter who had already reached late adolescence. The mother's habitual response to the daughter's efforts on all fronts was to point out how it could have been done better. To the daughter, who happened to be unusually intelligent and artistically talented, the prospect of making a career choice had already become a nightmare by the time she was a sophomore in college. In spite of abundant reassurance from peers and teachers, she could not believe that she was capable of making a sustained or successful effort in any direction, whether in art, which was her first choice, or in sociology, which was her second.

At an unconscious level, she correctly interpreted her mother's comments as warnings that if the daughter sought to set herself up as an individual separate from and rivalrous with her mother, the result would be rejection—not only emotional rejection but rejection of the daughter's claim to adequate functioning. The child kept begging for a kind of reassurance the mother could not give. A transfer of the parents out of the country finally presented the daughter with a crisis that was clear enough so that she could begin to come to grips with her panic about the future course of her own working life, but not before she had become frightened by the intensity of her own thoughts about suicide.

As in most cases, the issue here involved more than two family members; the father, through his passive withholding of support from either mother or daughter, left them in a state of continual vulnerability to each other, and made the daughter fearful that she must make a career choice only within the narrow parameters of the father's interests or she would lose him too. Rather than enter the danger zone of open dissension with father about what she was going to do with her life, the daughter was throwing herself into the impossible task of trying to reeducate him to a new set of values, then becoming covertly enraged because he would not or could not revise his view of the world. Her therapist was able to remind her that her father also was entitled to be himself and that the two of them could probably survive some disagreement with each other without losing each other entirely. The daughter was able to undertake the first steps toward disentangling her career concerns from her enmeshment with her mother and father, but the issue of her performance was still invested with a great deal of tension.

School phobia can be another instance of displacement by the child and other family members, the child's overt fear of school masking the mother's inability to separate from the child and the child's collusion in staying home. Here again, the child's performance becomes one of the first casualties. An adult's anxiety about going to work may have its roots in this dynamic.

Displacements that cause inhibitions of functioning in a child are not always a consequence of parent-child conflict or collusion; they can even result from misunderstanding. In one case, a 17-year-old came in because his parents were concerned about his underachievement in school. No evidence of learning disability could be found, and the boy and his parents appeared to be quite straightforward in their dealings with one another. The use of a genogram brought the nature of the difficulty to light. The father's younger brother had been a full-blown black sheep, getting into recurring difficulties with the law and with money, difficulties from which the grandfather and then the father kept bailing him out. About ten years ago, the father gave up trying and broke off contact with his younger sibling.

But the father could not break off the emotional ties that had held him and his brother together. Unable to help and convinced that further contact with his brother was futile, he became depressed. We can speculate that the depression might have had its original roots in the family difficulties that caused the brother to act as he did. At any rate, the 17-year-old had assumed from minor comments made by his father that he was responsible for his father's depression—that he had let his father down in some way that was causing his father pain. The son's distress was severe enough to impair his school performance, and it was not long before his father was indeed depressed about his son as well as about his brother, fearful that they would both turn out alike.

And to complete this vicious circle, the father began to convey his fearfulness to the son. Three further therapy sessions were enough to resolve the problem, but had it not been resolved, it could have cast a lasting pall over the growing son's efforts at individuation and career choice.

ANGRY REFUSALS

Occurring less frequently, but presenting a stiff challenge when it does occur, is the situation in which a child becomes so repelled by what one or both parents are doing as to repudiate them and refuse their guidance. The basis of the complaint could be social idealism; i.e., the child abhors what he or she perceives as the parents' uncaring materialism. Becoming acutely aware of the world's injustices and its uncompleted social tasks, the child may look with bewilderment at the parent who appears to believe that his or her identification with some corporate entity is reason enough for being. However, the parent, having struggled to get this far, may feel an inexpressible sense of pain at the child's rebuff. A son might be unnerved by the discovery that his father is alcoholic, unfaithful, engaged in corrupt practices at work, or some combination of these. Or it may be simply the degree of infantile conflict between the parents that the child finds intolerable. In these cases, whatever role in life the family has designated for the child, the child's response may escalate to the level of *angry refusal*, an active decision *to be against*, announced and defended with fervor, as if to surrender would mean a collapse of one's own emerging sense of self. Such an outcome was described in the first case in the section on joint displacements (p. 123).

The child may find some positive way to state the refusal, e.g., ''I think I will just stay in my job at the restaurant and skip college,'' but for many the refusal may take a diffuse oppositional form, e.g., ''I do not want to have to go through all the crap that it takes to get where you want me to go.'' The opposition may extend to a sense of disdain for whatever college has to offer, and if the person is enrolled in college the disdain may extend to what each teacher has to offer. Every demand from the world outside may be felt as an encroachment on some inner space which must be kept cleared in preparation for something, although the person's sense of what that something might be is shaped only by intuitions about what that something is *not*. Failure may be the only means the child has for expressing his or her protest against parental injustice. This of course can set a pattern that persists when the growing child enters the working world.

The cases in which the child chooses failure as a preferable option should not be confused with those in which the child holds back simply because he or she is afraid of failure.

In some cases, the opposition may have a more specific focus on the parent. If, for instance, it appears that the father has arrived at his present position by being ruthless with the people around him, then the fear of becoming identified with the father may lead the son or daughter to go to extremes of self-abnegation, even erupting with anxiety if they catch a glimpse of their father in their own performance. We described in Chapter 6 how the child, unable because of loyalty and fear to retaliate directly against the parent for abusive treatment, may displace that retaliation on someone else. If the child is aware of this impulse to retaliate against the parent and is struggling to restrain it, then the inhibition of his or her own functioning may become severe indeed.

TENSIONS RESULTING FROM WORK

So far our focus has been upon those tensions invading a person's performance because of the impact of previous generations on the person. The flow can, of course, go in the other direction; that is, stresses originating in work can also generate tensions between self and family. A great deal has been done within the field of industrial psychology to identify and evaluate such stresses, which may include work overload, overtime work, layoffs, transfers, irrational behavior of bosses, etc. These kinds of factors are mostly beyond the purview of this book. We wish, however, at least to touch upon some of the relational issues that can arise as the individual brings stress home from work, recognizing meanwhile that what the individual brought back from work might be partly a product of the expectations the individual took with him or her into the workplace.

The first of these issues involves the person who enters the work force with very high aspirations, one who may be called a self-elected "fast tracker." In our culture, we tend to think of this fast-moving individual as being exceptionally self-reliant; indeed, the very core of the ethos of the superstar is that he or she possesses magic powers of self-propulsion. Closer examination reveals that this is often a carefully nurtured image; everyone concerned, both in the corporation and in the family, is expected to attend to the nurturance. The bestowing of perks by the company must be timed so that they will turn up just when needed to foster the image: the layout and decoration of offices, the invitation to the company hunting lodge or to the box at the ball park, the use of the company jet, the introduction to the stock-sharing plan, etc. The family is also expected to contribute its part, with mother whispering to the children, "Don't disturb daddy, he has a lot on his mind." One of us saw an executive who, glancing at his watch as he sat down for his first and only interview, announced that he could take one hour to decide whether or not to divorce his wife. The paradox involved here is that this presumably *self*-propelled individual has in fact placed him- or herself in a state of *total dependency* on the willingness of the supporting cast to foster the image, to keep the fast track free of impediments. To the man engaged in the one-hour contemplation of divorce, for example, any deeper questions the therapist might raise about relational issues would seem to be out of order. In this context, the tension between self and family over performance involves the demands imposed upon everyone by the task of creating a superstar. Such demands can impose a severe imbalance on the ledger of relational accounts.

The other side of the picture involves the individual who, having aspired, has for some reason fallen short of expectations. This may be a person, for instance, who accepted the company's demands for total dedication and failed to develop any breadth of personal life interests—whose wife, for instance, might complain that her husband was unwilling to walk through an art gallery or even attend a Little League game. On arriving at early middle age, this individual might simply conclude that he or she had been had, that the rewards had not been commensurate with the sacrifices and nobody in the company was even bothering to keep score. The family is doubly ripped off, having for years held back their own demands, and now recognizing that the reward is going to be a crop of bitterness. It can be particularly painful when the bitterness is conveyed either through strident demands on the children to vindicate the parent's values through their own high achievement or, at the other extreme, through carping rejection of the children's efforts. In addition, there are the situations previously described in which the sense of frustration over career setbacks is expressed through condemnation of the spouse, in what at first appears to be a marital conflict.

A RELATIONAL PERSPECTIVE

In presenting this chapter on conflicts between self and family over performance, we do not mean to suggest that the working world is a briar patch where emotional forces originating in the family clutch at the individual and impede his or her every move. We do wish, however, to make the point that the cognitive and emotional readiness of an individual to achieve cannot be understood unless the complex variables of family process are taken into account. We believe this point has relevance to career counselors, therapists, and people concerned with the development of organizations.

It has equal relevance for those who are engaged in conflict between work and family, whether they are working with counselors or not. For the sources of conflict we are talking about involve relationships and relational imbalances, and for the participants the question of how to restore relational balance may be the crucial question of family life.

9

Entitlement: The Key to Career Growth

THE LINK BETWEEN CAREER ISSUES AND OTHER LIFE ISSUES

A Three-Way Struggle

Career issues are inextricably linked to other central life issues; and the life issue that is, from our perspective, most crucial in its impact on careers is the issue of entitlement.

We use the term *entitlement* in the sense formulated by Boszormenyi-Nagy (Boszormenyi-Nagy & Ulrich, 1981), and as such, entitlement has to do with a good deal more than the question of how individuals perceive themselves and their efforts. But we will begin with the question of self-perception.

This is complicated because the self is engaged in a three-way struggle, one that involves the work aspects of life as well as all the other aspects.

One aspect of the struggle is the tension that is generated between the members of the family of origin and the individual, due to the family's designation of who the individual is to be and what he or she is to do. The second aspect deals with the tension

131

between the individual and those others, whether nuclear family members or employers, who set up new expectations of what the person is to do. The third aspect involves the efforts of the individual to find room enough for an authoritative sense of self, a voice of one's own, a "zone of spontaneity."

This third aspect of the struggle is, of course, crucial. On the one hand, the person must deal with messages from the past that have to do with success and failure. On the other hand, sometimes the person must deal with ambiguous messages from the present dictating what and how one is to achieve. If one pursues the original mandates faithfully, this may readily lead one to feel like a failure or a fake in pursuing the dictates of the present or in seeking goals of one's own. If one pursues the dictates of the present, this may lead one to feel disloyal to the mandates of the past or a fake in relation to what one regards as one's true interests. The person may not seem to find much inside to sanction an entry into the zone of spontaneous self-directed functioning. As one man put it, "I've enjoyed my work, I'm not ashamed of it, but it's not who I am. Sometimes I feel like I'm sleepwalking, just putting on a performance. It gives me no peace of soul."

The Gap Between the Goals and the Realities

Until he was able to find a new occupation and lock a new perception of himself into place, the man whom we quote above had experienced periods of extreme discouragement, sometimes leading to depression. The gap between whatever is being sought after—whether the goal comes out of past designation, the demands of the present, or the inner voice of the self—and what has been realized can get so wide that the person suffers severe discouragement and a numbing sense that the self is worthless. This, we believe, is often the crucial therapeutic issue. What is at stake here, and what can be the target of therapeutic attention, is not simply what the person has done; it is the ongoing question of how the person *perceives* what he or she is doing in relation to various and *often conflicting* criteria.

THERAPEUTIC LEVERAGE: ENTITLEMENT

We believe the key to resolving the conflicts and moving on to new perceptions can be found in the concept of entitlement. In Chapter 3 on designation, we mentioned that some individuals seem to feel as if their entry into the world had not been marked by parental validation of their passport to existence. The therapist to whom we referred in that chapter could not *think* of herself as a therapist even though she had an active caseload. Strictly speaking, we do not believe the issue here is one of identity; we believe it can be described more accurately as a question of entitlement. Subjectively, the therapist did not *feel* entitled to function as a therapist or to consider herself as one. In other words, she did not feel that she had been given the permission or authority to function.

The Basis of Entitlement

From the point of view of basic ethical realities, a child possesses some entitlement simply by virtue of having been born. He or she is entitled to survival, care, and consideration. As a child grows and begins to perform in ways that are of value to the family (smiling being one of the earliest and most conspicuous), he or she may be said to have earned further entitlement. As the child continues to make contributions to the family and eventually to the world outside the family, his or her claim for return benefits becomes stronger. This does not mean that the child should be encouraged to demand tit for tat, a reward received for every task performed, but it does mean that his or her entitlement has expanded.

There may, however, be a gap of gigantic proportion between a child's subjective sense of entitlement, what he or she *feels* entitled to, and the objective reality of what that child's entitlement is. In a particular family, for instance, the older son may be designated to go out and succeed while the younger son may be designated to stand on the sidelines of life. Accordingly, the older son may *feel* a great deal more entitled than the younger, even without having done anything to earn it. Entitlement, by the way, can become a double-edged sword: the one who feels more entitled may reap some benefits from within the family, but the price he or she may have to pay in life in order to perform as designated, or the price of failing to perform, may be heavy in relation to the benefits received.

In terms of what he or she may actually have contributed to a family, on the other hand, a child's entitlement may be far in excess of what he or she perceives it to be. We have spoken of the debt of loyalty the child feels to the family based on having received life (see p. 34). As the parents provide care, the child may feel that what he or she owes the family is mounting up. The parents then may put an extreme demand on the child to make up for whatever they lack, when the child is still too young to know that what is being asked is way out of line. What the child does give to the family will contribute to the child's sense of having a valid claim for return benefits. But if there is still a gap between what the child can give and what the parents want, or what they appear to need, then the child, no matter how fervent his or her efforts, may continue to feel that he or she has not yet done anything on which to base a claim for return benefits. In the child's unconscious, the reasoning would go something like this: "If you can't cure your mother of her alcoholism, then what right have you got to think about being a writer?" The child feels restrained from making elective moves. It is as if the child, or the adult child, was not free to go off and start anything of his or her own choosing until all the duties to the family were done and the limitless debt written off.

When Acknowledgment Is Adequate

In many families, both the child's contribution to the family and the parents' acknowledgment of it may be quite adequate to leave the child unburdened by a sense of family debt as he or she matures. It is implicitly understood by everyone in the family that the child's contribution need not be as great as the parents' because the child will eventually grow up and provide parenting in turn. This may be directed toward children, aging parents, siblings, other relatives, or even other members of the community. Under these circumstances, a child may be expected to have an adequate sense of entitlement in two respects: the entitlement has been earned and the child has a subjective sense of possessing it.

When Acknowledgment Is Withheld

But the child who is designated to do some of the heavy work of the family, like absorbing disputes between the parents, may have earned an entitlement of which he or she remains altogether ignorant. While in fact the child may have given much, he or she may have been permitted by the parents, who are both the recipients and the scorekeepers, to feel that he or she can claim very little. This is like paying off a mortgage month by month without having the bank record your payments.

The sense of being without a valid claim can have a profound impact on expectations concerning work. In Chapter 3 we described the case of Edith, who, as a child, was told that she did not have the right to think, and who, as an adult, found that her achievements were sometimes accompanied by painful and disabling symptoms. She could not clearly claim credit for any of her achievements because she saw her movement through life as having been "horizontal," i.e., not rising to any heights of personal success. No matter what plaudits she might receive, no success would seem authentic until she dealt with the family issues that had caused validation to be withheld from her.

In another situation, a young woman who was about to receive her master's degree in counseling set out on her job search feeling "as if [she] were nothing." She could hardly bring herself to ask for a job interview. The fault was not with her training. She had been estranged from her father and stepmother for years, and she had hoped that her graduation would bring her back into the family. On receipt of her master's degree, she felt entitled to ask her parents if she could use the family's summer cottage, a request she had never dared make before. To her, their approval of this request would mean that she had become legitimate in their eyes. She heard the reply that it was full for the summer as a clear statement that the claim had been denied. If she had sought the master's degree primarily as a ticket of reentry into the family, she would now have to reexamine how the possession of this degree might help her arrive at a sense of entitlement without the family's assistance. In this case, as in so many others, to look at either the work or the personal aspect of this woman's life without taking the other into account would be like trying to play a piano sonata with one hand.

10

Therapeutic Strategies

Duly observing the law of parsimony, it makes sense at the beginning of therapy to see how far new clients can go by addressing the difficulties of the here and now. If the bonds of the past are going to interfere with therapeutic movement, this fact will emerge soon enough. Sometimes a rise in the pitch of one spouse's voice as he or she is halfway through a remark to the other spouse is all the clue a therapist needs that the strains of the past have been activated and will need to be explored. But our first concern is with therapeutic process in the here and now.

PART ONE: THE HERE AND NOW

The Balancing of Relationships

We think of therapy as designed to bring relationships into a fair balance of give-and-take through a process of negotiation. Various references to balancing have already been made in previous chapters. Let us make it clear that by balancing we do not have in mind the performance of a high-wire artist who must single-handedly manage the weights carried on either side. In human relationships, balancing is a reciprocal process; i.e., at least two players are required, and each must get adequate feedback from the other *before* trying to achieve a state of balance. We have had otherwise intelligent and sophisticated clients who had to be taught that instead of making a unilateral decision on a matter seriously affecting the spouse, they must open the decision-making process to the spouse if the decision is to work for the relationship.

Balancing male-female relationships. The most important balancing job in our society is the balancing of the interests of men and women. For a therapist dealing continually with marital and career issues, it is easy to forget how recently the issue of male-female balance has entered the national consciousness. As recently as 1979, an authoritative text on work stress omitted any reference to stress resulting from differential rewards for men and women (McLean, 1979). The emergence of this issue is, of course, the counterpart of the issue of the woman's role at home. It is now becoming apparent that among young people anticipating a working lifetime, the interests of males and females are quite similar. The old pattern of complementary roles seems to be shifting for most of us, and we are unprepared to adequately answer the question of how men and women are going to make room for each other.

Among our clients the question has a certain poignancy, as if both the men and the women feel that they are being asked to give up something dear to them. In one situation, an energetic lawyer/wife was trying to encourage her husband to be more outspoken about his needs, so that she would have time to decide how to respond to them, instead of being constantly caught off-guard. He freely acknowledged that it was hard for him to be direct; this was the result of a childhood of self-effacement. In fact, he said, he was at his friend Don's house last night and he really envied Don. Why? Because Don had shouted to his wife that he wanted a sandwich, and she promptly dropped what she was doing to make it for him. This, according to our client, was the kind of relationship he dreamed of.

"Yes," replied our client's wife, "I was talking to Don's wife this morning and she really was burned up about that sandwich. If she had a job of her own she would have had the nerve to tell him to make it himself." So much for our client's dreams!

Needless to say, in seeking a balance with men, our female clients are forced to give up the illusion that men can guarantee their security. Yet, in the workplace, the rapid emergence of women into equal or superior roles gives both men and women, if they are willing to utilize it, an unprecedented opportunity to know one another on relatively equal and open terms. This can provide a new foundation for appreciation, even admiration. At a case conference not long ago one of us observed that men had become bereft of women's admiration, which they used to get and still needed. In response to this, a female colleague replied, "Perhaps women will now be able to find things in men that they can really admire." Part of the challenge of developments like these, of course, is that they can and will eventually take place without being thrown off course by currents of sexual interest. But the arrival at new understandings, and the fair allocation of what is onerous and what is rewarding, will not occur on any kind of hit-or-miss basis. The establishment, for example, of the Dual Career Workshop at the Harvard Business School, as described by Day in the *Harvard Business School Bulletin* (1985), is an example of conscious effort directed toward the goal of balance.

The work of balancing will not, of course, resemble a legalistic process in which the terms of give-and-take are inflexible. This work will reflect the changing needs of men and women as they progress through their individual life cycles in the context of the family life cycle. As Portner (1983) observed, a woman who considers herself devoted to work may find that she wishes to shift her devotion to having a family instead, and this matter becomes part of the ongoing dialogue with the spouse. The process of negotiation needs to occur whenever a relationship lasts long enough so that individual interests have to be fit together.

Changing intergenerational relationships. Like husband-wife relationships, parent-child relationships are shifting; as the child is

flooded with outside influences and pressures, the parent is compelled to allow the child more room to explore. It requires the
parent being more highly skilled in maintaining sufficient control while still permitting movement and growth. As parents live
longer, there is also the complex task of sorting out the rights
and interests of adult children and their aging parents. New opportunities offer themselves for conflict as well as for growth and
reconciliation. The adult who can negotiate effectively enough
so as to balance the claims of self, work, and family has reached
a position in life that we might venture to call, "grown up."

Negotiation: Our Meaning

Negotiation as power. As used in this context, the term *negotiation* has a specific meaning. We are not using it as in some union-
management negotiations where the negotiator is, in the strictest
sense, an advocate and an adversary whose job is to get the best
possible terms for the client, assuming that the opposing parties
will have to look out for themselves. In other words, we are not
referring to a unilateral move, based on power, to position one's
self as the continual winner regardless of the impact on the other.
Nor are we dealing with that variety of "assertiveness," sometimes espoused by feminists and macho males, that requires the
militant pressing of one's own interests until one's own position
is firmly established, *before* taking the other's interests into account, a point that never seems to be reached.

Communication. A clear distinction may also be made between
what we are talking about and *communication*. It is, of course, good
for husbands and wives to be able to talk about their thoughts and
feelings with each other. This kind of expression can be crucial
to a marriage. However, the act of "spilling out" can become an
endless, pointless reweaving of the same old tapestry when it
is allowed to substitute for the effort required to identify issues,
be accountable for one's own part in them, and resolve them.
When this kind of substitution takes place, a passionate dedication to "communication" may serve as a total cop-out. And, if

the push is toward full disclosure, it can destroy the relationship, as it sometimes does.

Focus on issues. In this context negotiation is an issue-focused process. Whether the people involved are assisted by a therapist or are undertaking this kind of dialogue on their own, the first task, and sometimes the hardest, is to identify the issue.

Fairness. In the negotiating process, a good deal of attention may be paid to how people are feeling. But this is not just for the sake of going through a catharsis. It is because feelings provide a sensitive gauge of whether or not an individual perceives something as fair. We see fairness as the basic criterion for the resolution of issues because this seems to us to be the essence of what people are seeking. What permits people spontaneously to mobilize their energies is often the sense that they can put trust in the response to their efforts. What is fair cannot, of course, be stated by one party. It can emerge only out of the working through of differing points of view.

We hope it is clear that we are not out to sell some kind of magic whereby people can automatically expect a trusting response to their trusting overtures. What we are suggesting is that people can be alert for possibilities of reciprocal trust-building, and when a relationship built on reciprocal trust is achieved, it can serve as the hub of a widening network of people building connections.

How the Process Works

Defining issues. In practice it often proves to be extraordinarily difficult even to identify an issue. A wife, for example, may try to talk to her husband about the amount of time he spends at work. Her unacknowledged fear may be that he has lost interest in the marriage, while his may be that his manhood will be threatened if he permits his spouse to influence his decisions about his work. Rather than risk a confrontation over this latent agenda, each may assist the other without conscious intention in simple diversionary measures such as endless point-blank disagreements about how often the husband has been late getting home. But if there is a need for further distance from the topic, the wife may shift to her having trouble with the children during the dinner hour because he does not support her discipline, or the husband to her demands about their life-style. If the particular issue can be hidden under a flurry of counterissues, then there is little risk of any real movement toward changes that could be unsettling or possibly devastating. What he will carry back to work is merely his resentment at her for interfering; the question of how they are going to balance his work demands with their needs as a family may never get aired.

As Bowen (1978) has suggested, the dyadic relationship is inherently unstable, and when there is stress a third party will be drawn in. It takes some effort and discipline for two people to stay with an issue; it is usually the path of least resistance to topple off the real issue into a safety net of defensive substitutes.

Negotiating the issues. Presenting points of view can be a lengthy process even if there are no interruptions; each person will usually want to rebut the other(s) and make further points, which may serve either to clarify or obscure the issue. The process of "multidirectional siding," described at length elsewhere (Boszormenyi-Nagy & Ulrich, 1981), enables the therapist to permit all the involved parties to make their claim, as well as to require them to make it clearly. The therapist usually has to work hard to help the family members reach the point where they all can see what the consequences of a decision might be. The objective here is for the concerned parties to be able to lay out all of the facts relevant to an outcome, each being attentive enough to the others so that gradually everyone begins to see the whole picture instead of just a fragment. This can lead to productive shifts in outcome: A prenegotiating position (husband to wife): "You don't want my daughters playing with our baby because you just want to boss everybody." An evolving position: "I understand your concern about their dropping the baby on its head, but it seems to me that you could be more relaxed during their visits."

The negotiating process can lead to varying kinds of outcomes. There may be a need for further preliminary work: "I could be more relaxed with your daughters if you didn't automatically take their side about everything." There may be an agreed-upon delay: "This is too hot to handle now, let's table it till after your sister leaves." Or there may be a clear-cut decision: "The purchase of the house can be delayed a week while we hunt for one you like better," "I will change my plans so I can stop off at your mother's," etc.

In this kind of negotiating, a concession can be a gift of caring; as such, it can provide a way for both parties to move ahead. Successful resolution of each issue adds to the relationship. If a couple can move from defensive mistrust to active sharing of concern, then the payoff from negotiating has transcended the immediate issue.

Of course, negotiations can stall, with each person dug into an unyielding position. The therapist will then have to help each assess the actual costs of holding out.

> Your fights about how to manage the girls do not show a genuine concern over child guidance. You are exploiting the children in these fights with each other over turf. If you keep on this way, you could quickly drive the children off and ruin the marriage. You have to decide whether it is worth it.

Families that are beginning to get the knack of looking at issues may show a gradual progression from peripheral to central concerns, waiting for enough trust to build up so they can tackle the big ones. The movement over time might be from deciding where to spend the weekend, to the decision whether to bring an aging parent into the household instead of a nursing home.

Attempting to balance interests. In the following example, a husband and wife look at a career crisis of hers and at how they can handle this issue together. He has a good corporate job but his salary did not cover her expenses at graduate school, so he has been selling stocks on a falling market. Layoffs are occurring in his department. She does not want to return to her old work but is very doubtful that she can get a job in her new field. The therapist asks the husband how he sees this situation. From his initial response, it is clear that the husband wants his wife to give up and go back to her old job, but he does not want to face what this means.

Husband: There must be a way you can make a decision like that and feel great about it.

Wife: If I don't take the old job, he'll hound me.

Husband: It does seem premature to stop trying—but if it's a choice between the old job or nothing?

Wife: The worst is doing nothing.

Therapist: Where do you think he's coming from?

Wife: It sounds like he's moving in too much. But he's been paying my way. So I can allow his getting into it.

Husband: Sixty percent of the people in my department are out. Great people. I have a fearful feeling about my own job. I want *her* to feel the concern.

Therapist: Do you?

Wife: I do, I'm aware of the risk. I realize that he's not just getting even with me, it's not personal.

Husband: She does accuse me of leaning on her, and then I bite back. But the real great part comes from the feeling that we can face it together.

Wife: I have a very negative feeling about staying home and doing nothing. Like, washing your underwear, it's not something I can get better at. But I really don't want to do the old job. I think I've decided not to do it, I hope to get something in the new field, I'll take a chance.

Therapist: Are you ready for her to make a decision?

Husband: It's good to make a choice.

Wife: Till today, I thought he was leaning on me. Now I see his real fears and his concern and sense of responsibility.

Husband: You're making the decision, and it's not an easy one for me to feel good about. But I don't like her feeling pressured or being leaned on any more than she does now. It's a rotten feeling.

Wife: I can see it in different terms now.

Thus they negotiate her career status while examining their negotiations. Each is arriving at a decision that involves awareness of the other's interests. She is freer to go ahead; her acknowledgment of his fear makes it easier for him to join her in facing the risks.

Breakdown

The process. We have observed how easy it is for those involved in negotiating to fall back on defensive strategies. As this happens, very rapid escalation may occur, which appears to go along with quite rapid regression for whomever is involved. Suspicion emerges and anger mounts. If the anger becomes hot enough, the suspicion may sound quite paranoid. The suspicion activates fear. Each person may begin to feel that his or her position is so badly threatened that the only possible defense is to destroy the position of the adversary, even if this means destroying the adversary. As each person begins to get the desperate sense that something he or she values greatly is about to be damaged or destroyed, "deafness" may set in. It may take the therapist a while to realize that the person is not hearing.

The more intelligent the persons so engaged, the more devastating their attack can get. The more narcissistic they are, the more sensitive they are to the attack. One of the most vigorous exercises in which a therapist can engage is tackling two intelligent, narcissistic people who appear to be trying to reduce each other to shreds over a domestic issue, a mode of attack that can be called *image bashing*. They can sometimes be brought to a halt if compelled to see what they are doing to each other. One couple backed off from further fights only after an incident in which she tried to scratch his face while he was driving on the thruway. Her account of it was that at that point she finally got scared.

Another wife reported that at the climax of a violent argument, her husband "saw where [they] were going and began to stop, and [she] was able to follow him." His response: "Now that we have learned how to do that on the smaller issues, we will be able to start dealing with the big ones."

Where is the fulcrum? Even when the partners in the balancing process have serious intentions and are trying to work at it, the process can break down. The following example of failed negotiation is also the life story of two people who were far enough apart to experience a good deal of pain.

Husband: Thirteen years ago I said I didn't want to be sales VP of Extec. Life is too short. You mature with the passage of time, you begin to realize, "I don't want to do *that*." The price is too high, the interference with your personal life. I don't want that. I also believe there is a fundamental balancing problem. You have to find—it's a tremendous battle. There are pressures on both sides. You try to find some reasonable medium. It's been that way my whole life, I talked of it in college. It was bad enough then. Then with kids and everything—you recognize it's a balancing act. What you're trying to figure out is, where the hell is the fulcrum?

Wife: At home it didn't come through that way. I only saw the 85 percent of you going into your work. I didn't see the struggle to balance. You never saw Ted's teacher for four years in high school. How important is Ted's career in high school versus Extec? That's the kind of thing that lays heavy on people's minds.

Husband: I'm trying to say that's part of the balancing act.

Wife: It looked to the family like we got the short end of the stick.

Therapist: What do you think of what he just said?

Wife: I was aware of words but not actions.

Husband: I know that's how you feel, but it has no acknowledgment that—you don't see the side I walk away from. She can't be expected to see it. It's just a fact.

Therapist: It looks like there are two sets of books, with no connections.

Wife: We weren't silent, but we weren't communicating. I heard it as words, not actions. My comprehension of what the words meant wasn't on the same scale as his.

Husband: When *you* went to work you began to see what work pressure meant. And that's *nothing*, compared to what I went through. In my kind of job the commitment is *indefinite*. You're still working for somebody else. Even if you're a high-level exec you still don't control your own calendar. The culture at Extec is uniquely frenetic. Everybody understands that, even the guys at IBM. It's in the environment. Many of us have been trying for years to change it. It has to rub off on her, it's gotta be a factor, but there's not much she can do about it.

Therapist: It's hard to do the books on this marriage.

Husband: As the situation has gotten better, her anger has not diminished. As if it's an outgrowth of something before. That's a real concern to me. That's the frustration of it, and I begin to say, what the hell.

Therapist: Are there specific things that can be addressed now?

The couple goes on to look at specific issues together. Evidently the wife has heard something in what her husband said, because she says she feels closer to him now, and she has some hope that things will be all right. In spite of all the missed connections, the evidence of his concern is important. If the "outgrowth of something before" can be brought under control, there is still the possibility of new growth in the here and now.

PART TWO: A MULTIGENERATIONAL APPROACH

Sometimes attention to the here and now is sufficient to satisfy the goals of therapy. Sometimes, "outgrowths of something before" and the factors responsible for those outgrowths get in the way. Then it is necessary to find out why the bonds of the past hold people back from making the changes they want. We tend to view this question in terms of conflict between designation and self-validation.

In order to have the freedom to arrive at validation of the self, one must work loose the existing bonds of designation. And since designation comes out of the convergence of multigenerational forces, we believe that a multigenerational approach is necessary if people are to work toward having that freedom. There is no "magic bullet" approach to the validation of one's claims in life, but therapy, properly focused, can assist the process. Effective therapeutic work on the bonds of designation means tracing the roots of designation in the multigenerational history of the family. When the client has a solid grasp of how the power of designation has affected his or her actions during critical life events, then therapeutic leverage is available to work at new responses, provided this is done without destroying the person's loyalty to the origins of the family.

One client, for instance, reported that he had an acute concern about being "Wonder Boy" in the eyes of everyone important to him, which simultaneously meant being very careful not to make mistakes. This put him in a bind that interfered with dates, sibling contacts, and his attempts at remaining calm in his dealings with his boss. He could not understand why such concerns should intrude when basically he thought well enough of himself. The tracing of multigenerational patterns brought to light a number of designating factors; e.g., the client's own caution about making mistakes mirrored the caution of his father, who had been clearly designated as "mama's boy" and had learned always to play it safe. But the central theme appeared in the mother's family; in response to the demands under which she grew up, the mother had an omnivorous, narcissistic hunger that required her to examine her sons almost hourly to make sure that they were ready to pass inspection by her family. The exploration of this intense need of the mother's had to be conducted with empathy for her if the client's loyalty to her was to be supported.

It was this ravenous hunger in the people around him that the client was attempting to satisfy. Keeping everybody fed without making any mistakes was, to say the least, strenuous. Not too surprisingly, it turned out that his boss and his longtime girlfriend were both people who demanded continual feeding. His girl-friend's need for understanding and support seemed insatiable as she engaged in marathon monologues about the conflicts she was having with her parents and with people at work. And his boss had a knack for catching him at five o'clock and requesting instant memoranda on matters that could obviously wait. Or the boss would fly into a frenzy over minutiae, even flaring up at a misplaced comma. The client reported, "My first reaction was absolute fear. What would happen if he *really* blew? I had to work very hard to contain my feelings." It became evident that the client unconsciously felt responsible for preserving his boss's sanity by avoiding mistakes that would push his boss over the edge. A little further exploration revealed that the boss, rather than being provoked to a frenzy by the client, was picking up his frenzy somewhere else and using the client's actions to justify it. Rather than provoking his boss, the client was simply giving him a safety valve. This too, of course, was a kind of feeding.

Within weeks after recognizing what a hold such demands had on him, the client had found a new girlfriend with whom he felt quite relaxed. He also was beginning to assess whether or not he wished to go on meeting his boss's demands. Facing this issue produced new anxieties. What is especially significant about such responses to treatment is that change can occur more or less simultaneously in one's working life and one's personal life, in-dicating that interrelated processes are involved.

The Realistic Assessment of Debt

Designation consists of a set of demands upon the person by the family that can be characterized as debts to the family that one is expected to pay. Once it has been determined clearly what these debts are, then an objective assessment of what a person has *already paid* into the family may relieve some of the pressure for further giving. It is not uncommon, for instance, for someone to recall with real distress that they were only a nuisance, or worse, to their family, only to have careful exploration bring to light that their behavior served to distract the parents from their own battles or to bring them back from their depressive involvement with themselves. Often an adult will attach no meaning to past efforts made on behalf of the family, such as taking care of younger siblings or helping to fill, for each parent separately, the void left by divorce. It is useful for the therapist to find out about and give due recognition to the performance of such tasks, e.g., being the family nuisance or sibling-sitter, for this kind of recognition can genuinely reinforce the sense that one has discharged at least part of one's debt and is free to make some claims of one's own.

The assessment of what one still *realistically* owes the family can also reinforce the sense that one's own claims have some validity; what was before a matter of endless obligation can now become a matter of give-and-take. Freed from a sense of total obligation, the daughter who regularly made two long round trips by car to pick up and return her mother can reasonably ask mother to come across Long Island Sound on the ferryboat for her weekly visits. In contrast, an unreal debt might, for instance, consist of a deeply imbedded conviction that as long as the mother is depressed, the daughter should give mother her primary attention no matter what the cost to her own life. The attempt to pay this unbounded debt could leave the daughter exhausted, whereas recognition of what she realistically owes would leave her free to invest her energy elsewhere. One client reported how as a young adult he had gotten tired of his father's asking for repayment, requested that his father present him with a bill for the balance due on their accounts, paid it in cash, and walked off feeling like a free man—without losing contact with his father.

Of course with this kind of reduction of responsibility there may come onslaughts of anxiety and depression, because to revise the basic terms of designation means that the old contract is broken, the old fantasied true love from an approving parent will never be won—the existential gap between parent and child will have to be recognized. This gap can be overcome to some extent if the spirit of give-and-take, of ongoing negotiation of balances between parent and child, can be generated. Some parents respond to their adult child's efforts at opening up new channels, others see the child's attempts as just one more annoying example of what was wrong with him or her in the first place. Some parents are even willing to do some reworking of the past as well as of the present, e.g., giving acknowledgments of the child's merit that had previously been withheld. In the case of the young man who paid back his father, this freed them to have a new kind of man-to-man relationship with each other around business issues, and the son did very well in business. Yet because of the father's pride and reticence they were never able to discuss what had separated them emotionally as father and son; the son continued to feel the emotional gap, and this, in turn, affected his fathering.

Refusal to Accept Payment

The assessment of what is truly owed can take on a sad aspect if the creditors block payment. In one case, a daughter, her husband, and three small children would arrive at her parents' farm after a five-hour drive from the city only to be greeted, not by suitable hellos, but by a hastily mumbled, "Well, come in, we have to get out to our chores." The five-hour drive did not give the daughter a claim to a warm welcome, nor did any of her other efforts win her any consideration. To meet her parents' terms, the daughter would at least have had to give up her "fat city" life-style, replace the husband with somebody local, and try to be about ten years younger. At every turn, in other words, it seemed as if her parents were saying to her, "Get back inside the parameters where you belong, and then we'll see."

In this case it must be apparent that we are not presenting an empathic view of the parents. When parents such as these show every indication of being impossible to reach, a special and extraordinary effort is required of both the clients and the therapist in order to see the parents in a human light, sometimes calling for an imaginative leap a client is not yet ready to make.

In a milder case, the parent may start a phone call from the grown child with, "Why didn't you call sooner?" Or a father cannot see why his son does not send postcards during his business trips to Hong Kong. Such complaints can serve to keep the offspring off balance, never sure when they have done enough, never sure where to draw the line, never sure when they can go out to play—or work—with a true feeling of being on their own. The parents' fear of their own obsolescence may be a major stumbling block in the way of their being able to acknowledge the valid claim of the offspring to an independent existence.

In the case of parental refusal to accept what can be offered, an alteration of circumstances may open new doors. A young woman who for years was conscious only of hatred for her mother, and who could not get her mother to accept anything worth having, found that she was able to restore the relationship to some extent by nursing the mother during her terminal illness. This added immeasurably to the daughter's own sense of wholeness and value. Perhaps by coincidence, she began to move upwards rapidly out of a stagnant entry-level job.

Balancing Debts to the Dead

Even if the death of a parent puts a stop to efforts at getting things into balance, it is still possible to build entitlement and work to overcome the uneasy sense of indebtedness by taking measures toward the recognition and exoneration of the parent. The simple act of obtaining a proper headstone for a grave could be such a measure, or a search through old letters that might account for a parent's failures. There can be a direct connection between such efforts and the liberation of energy for improved functioning at work.

Exoneration

In our approach to the reworking of entitlements there is an inherent paradox. The therapist may easily see the parents of the clients as perpetrators of injustice, while being compelled to recognize that the parents were themselves victims. The recognition of this paradox is vital if this kind of therapy is to succeed. The client will earn no validation by adopting the view that his or her parent was no good and therefore not worth the benefit of any feeling of obligation. The bonds of obligation cannot be shrugged off.

In one case, a client described how her childhood efforts at cutting through her parents' arbitrary unfairness were routinely dismissed by the parents as being confused, crazy, and irrational. Under these circumstances the girl did indeed sometimes get emotional, and this led her to believe that her parents were right.

A previous therapist, in reviewing these childhood scenes with the client, had explained them something like this: "Don't you see, you were OK, it was your parents who had the problem?" As it usually does, this explanation had left our client in a bind. Trying to close the books on the affair by attributing all the craziness to the parents did not afford her much relief. Instead, it left her feeling that she had sought to vindicate herself at the cost of wiping out her parents' positions. Our knowledge of the basis of relationships tells us that if the position of the parents is destroyed, the child is quite likely to tumble into the void along with the parents.

To get at the heart of the matter, it was necessary for our client to do the hard work of figuring out what it was about the parents that had led them to be so grossly unjust to her. This would help to restore her sense of their humanness. When no longer paralyzed by the fear of them or by the shock of rejecting them, our client could begin to take a realistic look at what she was entitled to claim of them. She could legitimately claim, after all, to have a good mind, capable of lucid thoughts about who was being unfair to whom. Since she happened to be a trial lawyer, this capacity was useful in her work.

The exonerative task described above may sound familiar because so many people do it on their own accord. Until this process has occurred, whether in or outside of therapy, the individual is not free to throw off the bonds of designation.

Facing the Self

For some people it seems as if the hardest part of all is simply recognizing themselves. Facing the denied facts about one's own resources—denied because they did not fit within the designated parameters—can be unbelievably difficult. Or the facts can be acknowledged but there may still be a sense of paralysis about acting on them. Or they may be acted on, only to have the action or its results be described as meaningless. Just when a crucial trial action is taking place, such as applying for a new job, the client may present the therapist with such a fit of despair as to make the treatment seem hopeless. Nevertheless, new actions can be gradually tested out until the person reports that they do have meaning. What was unthinkable or swathed in confusion before, can now acquire clarity: This is me, and I am doing this, and it is good after all.

Altering the Balances

Change in one's own functioning alters the balance between the self and significant others. We have already spoken of re-working the balance with parents; as this frees a person for change, new accommodations with other people start to take place. The release from old bonds that triggers new confidence at work may also trigger a realization that one is tired of playing the old image-bashing games with one's partner. The need to use the partner as a substitute victim, or to be used as such, may have dwindled. The time comes to call for clarity about who really owes what to whom. There may be new guidelines to work out about lovemaking, caring for the children, visiting relatives, house-keeping, or spending money. As the debt to the family of origin is reduced, then more may be available for one's spouse, one's work, one's children, and one's community, as well as one's self, and thought will have to be given to the distribution. The pro-cess of negotiating the balance never stops.

When husband and wife have shown that they have built enough reciprocal trust so they can carry on the negotiating pro-cess without help from the therapist, this is probably the time for therapy to stop.

Looking at Work Issues

One of the major issues that may arise in therapy is whether there are family pressures pushing the client to make nonsyntonic choices regarding work. It may prove desirable to do a careful exploration of what the family has designated for the person, while simultaneously exploring expressions of spontaneous interest. An individual designated to play a cautious, somewhat subservient role might have fantasies about breaking away into some entirely new venture of his or her own. Further reflection might show that the intense pressures of getting such a venture off the ground would probably conflict with the person's enjoyment of low-keyed mentor relationships with subordinates, so that the ideal role might be one in which the person could exercise authority in a small existing company; however, such reflection might serve only to perpetuate for a little while longer the denial of a real wish to be on one's own.

Sometimes the most pertinent aspects of family designation may take a long time to surface. An individual who felt extreme ambivalence about completing his doctoral dissertation had been in treatment for nearly a year before he could bring up the fact that his family had expected his older brother, who died soon after graduation from college, to be the Ph.D. holder of the family.

The other major issue concerning work that may arise in therapy is whether patterns carried over from the family are shaping the person's adaptation to work. If, for instance, a client reports an intense visceral reaction to an irrational piece of behavior by the boss, it is appropriate to explore whether the client ever experienced such a reaction in a family setting. Sometimes a very specific precursor may be found that will provide a natural shift from work to family issues; sometimes it may be necessary to work with family issues for a while before the precursor comes to the surface.

Once the pattern has been identified, it becomes an easy matter to look at a person's current response to work in the light of the old responses. A man whose attempts at taking care of his alcoholic father had ended abruptly one day when the father told the son to get out of his life and stay out, was quite sensitive to anything that seemed like a rebuff from his boss—so sensitive, in fact, that he was continually on the verge of offering to quit.

Much working through can be done of these kinds of fears and anxieties arising out of the family. When the apparently irrational behavior of a boss sets an old pattern in motion, a related line of inquiry is whether this extends to the person's relationships with peers and subordinates, in accordance with the dictates of the old family pattern.

Essentially this therapeutic effort has to do with discovering and then renegotiating the old terms that governed one's life within the family, in order to liberate one's self for spontaneous dealings in the present. As soon as this process begins, it changes the balance in the here and now so that new negotiations are called for. The effort required to clarify the terms of designation, to renegotiate them, and to start work on new balance can seem heroic, and the leverage provided by a career counselor working with the therapist can be of real value in this process, as the case of Kay in Chapter 11 will illustrate.

11

Good Old Kay

The case of Kay demonstrates the intergenerational force of designation, a force strong enough to be almost like a physical barrier against which Kay had to throw herself again and again in her struggle to find and claim a sense of herself.

THE PRESENTING ISSUE: A FAILING MARRIAGE

The case began with a visit from Kay's husband, Jim, who was concerned about his wife's depression:

> She's sad all the time, sad and very insecure. She's disturbed . . . she can't handle being alone, she wants lots of talk and reassurance and intimacy with me, but it doesn't do any good and anything can touch her off. I got home twenty-five minutes late the other night and all hell broke loose. Kay blew up, she threw things, she hit me . . .

This was Jim's second marriage—he had boys 23, 18, and 16 from the first—but it was Kay's first marriage, and their first child had arrived eight months prior to Jim's decision to seek profes-

sional help. Kay and Jim had been married eight years, but after
a one- or two-year honeymoon period, pressures had started to
build until Jim reached the point where he felt lost, with no idea
how to help his wife or where to turn.

Kay came in with Jim for the second session and confirmed
everything he had reported, adding that she felt they were very
near the end of their marriage. "Any little thing sets off an ex-
plosion in me," she said, "and suddenly I'm screaming and yell-
ing and I can't stand it." The whole thrust of her complaint was
that she could not trust Jim to act as if anything she said or did
had any importance.

> I've always been important till something else comes along.
> There's no teamwork, his attitude is "don't bother me," and
> he either leaves things undone or does them all by himself and
> leaves me out. What effort he does make is artificial, he does
> not deal with me emotionally.

Jim showed great strain in his response to Kay. He freely con-
ceded that he procrastinates. "I put her last, I put her off till she
hits the fan. I'm scared, I do play games with her and she spots
it every time." Hanging his head and hanging his hands between
his knees, Jim said miserably, "I need to train myself to talk to
her, to listen, to be more intense." Evidently this was a grim
prospect.

Kay showed no sympathy for Jim. "The only way I can get
a reaction is to threaten. It makes a monster out of me. I hate who
I am. I feel forced into acting like his first wife, she threatened
him too. I can't believe it."

As Kay in one session after another spelled out the monstrosity
of what was happening, Jim would finally come to his own
defense. If we put his remarks together, it comes out like this:

> I'm always busy putting out fires with the job and the kid. I
> resent taking time from work, my work is sliding. I can focus
> on her for three days, then I goof on day four and she yells
> all day. On a scale of one to ten I'm an eight, I do help. But
> if I deviate, the penalties are too harsh. She's very bitter, she

feels she's being cheated. But what's her standard of comparison? It's a mystery to me.

It appeared that control was part of the issue. "She tries to teach me to get things done. She put up a blackboard. I don't want her to take charge of everything, I feel she's asking me to give up myself. I used to argue with her, but she always wants to do it her way." To this Kay would reply, "I'm not allowed to be right." From the initial impression of a wife prostrated by her husband's passivity, the picture was shifting: Kay appeared to have a great deal of energy but most of it was tied up in her conflict with Jim. In our experience, when spouses give contradictory accounts of their lives together, attempts to unscramble the facts lead nowhere, and the conflicting information can be taken only as evidence of how the protagonists feel toward each other. In this case, they seemed to feel such determination to disagree that we were apparently at an impasse.

BEYOND THE MARRIAGE: THE EMERGENCE OF ISSUES ABOUT SELF AND WORK

During the first session, Jim had mentioned in passing that Kay was a pro in the financial world, but she dropped out and did not want to go back to it. A month later he came back to this theme: "She let a career pass her by. She gives her friends advice. She got too involved in my job. She can't live through me, there's no future in it." The cumulative effect was to portray a person who had been quite active.

During the first two months, Kay used her sessions to repeat her litany of how Jim let her down. Jim meanwhile seemed steeped in gloom at the prospect of how he would have to change himself in order to change the marriage. The therapy, like the marriage, would have seemed at an impasse, except for the series of references Jim had made to Kay's activities. The amount of energy Kay demonstrated while expanding her litany, in spite of her avowedly depressed state, made it seem plausible that she had indeed had energies available in the past for more productive activity. Even though Kay expressed her crisis in terms of her marriage, it began to appear that there were matters outside the marriage that were worth looking at and that we would not be able to get beyond the present impasse until we did so.

We began wider explorations, and it soon became clear that the sense of hopelessness permeated Kay's life. In terms of the immediate present, she described how she had come to a standstill: "I hate to clean house. It's draining to be by myself in the house. I'm wasting time, I don't function. Nothing gets done." Kay also began talking about present and past relationships with members of her own family. Here too the sense of hopelessness emerged. Once it was clear to Kay that the therapist would help her talk about things outside the marriage, she was able to acknowledge, "Ever since I met Jim, his schedule became my schedule. I changed my whole world for him. I fell in the pit. *My depression is that I let this happen.*"

Concurrently with this shift in treatment, specifics emerged about Kay's working life. After merchandising school, she had started as a buyer at Gimbel's and when that wore thin she switched to managerial work and was soon in charge of four departments. When she saw this was going nowhere, she got a job with an investment service. She was selling the investment service to investment bankers, and although, when she began, she "didn't know a stock from a bond," within three years her earnings with commissions went over thirty thousand dollars. As she described these events, Kay might as well have been talking about selling doughnuts, for all the feeling she showed.

How had she gotten from there to here? She gave up the selling job because she was tired of it. She also expected to become pregnant, although this actually did not occur for several years. Now she has no idea at all what she would do if she were to return to the job market.

On the surface, these facts might have seemed plausible as an account of how Kay had come to her present impasse. But by now it was obvious that the reasons for Kay's sense of hopelessness were not going to be found on the surface. Her dilemma could not be dismissed simply as the blocking of a career by the

conventional demands of marriage, because some of the surrender took place before the marriage, and in her remarks about
her family, cues were emerging about what had gone wrong. In-
tensive exploration of the part Kay played in her family of origin
was begun.

KAY'S CHILDHOOD

Kay was the middle child of five, with two older sisters and
a younger sister and brother, all about a year apart. In recon-
structing the story of her childhood, Kay told how the family had
experienced hardship because her father, whose ability enabled
him to obtain good editing jobs, let his anger separate him from
one job after another. And although her mother worked, they
still struggled to make ends meet. Her mother taught them all
how to cope—by sticking together as a family unit. "In my family,
family came first, things were handled together." The children
pitched in, earned their own money, wore each other's clothes.
"You expected to give—you did not expect a return." Not only
did Kay eventually put herself through college, but her mother
used some of Kay's college loan money to help the others through
school. Resentment was out of the question; it was understood
that the family depended on individual sacrifices for its survival.
"We always kept the trust." Her mother was not arbitrary about
how she shifted the resources around in the family; she tried to
make it come out fair for everybody. She would, for instance,
give everyone identical gifts for Christmas.

The Care of Father

Heavy as the economic burden was, Kay's major part in the
family did not have to do with economics. Her father was "nerv-
ous"—he would let things work on him and finally he would
"flip out"; his wrath was devastating, especially to her mother.
Kay found that her task was to cater to her father, to be cheerful, to be "good old Kay," but otherwise to stay as anonymous
as she could, to avoid provoking him. Being anonymous meant,

among other things, not having problems of her own. Her efforts were not purely selfless; she yearned for a response when
she smiled, but there were no return smiles, no benefits. As Kay
saw it later, her efforts to keep the peace, to avoid making waves,
to keep a smile on her face, meant having no identity of her own.
"I was able to get by on that."

There was no complaining to her mother about her father. Her
mother left no doubt about her basic tenets, which included the
following: "You father has his troubles, but he is a good man."
Kay accepted her mother's belief that her father was a good man
at the core. But having to take his heavy-handed treatment without complaint made his goodness hard to swallow.

Mother's Self-Denial

Her mother's defense of her father was part of her own self-
lessness. When she lit the marriage candle at the altar and ex-
tinguished the candle representing herself, she meant it. She rarely did anything that anyone could interpret as being for herself;
and when she did, it was only if she had arrived at a valid excuse. One did not "go shopping"; one might pause at the store
on the way home from a visit to a sick friend.

Commitment to the Trust

Reflecting on her attempts to initiate activities outside the family, Kay said, "We were never motivated into anything." She won
a trophy in track, but it was "no big deal" to the family, and
she did not continue to compete. "I don't know if mother even
knew I didn't go back." By this time it had become ingrained
in Kay that her energies belonged to the family.

As an adolescent, she dreamed that she would have something
better than her sisters. She would not be just a housewife. There
was no doubt in her mind about that.

But whatever she was going to be, to have, to do, did not
emerge in college. There she felt insecure, nobody tried to help,
she "just hid." The post-college choice of merchandising school

was not Kay's bid for the future; it was her mother's notion of how to get ready to have something to fall back on if the need arose—i.e., if Kay got married and her husband could not provide for her.

During the early working years, Kay, as the only daughter without children, found her mother expecting her home weekends. "I ran home to take care of them." Her father was ill, and since illness made him angrier, Kay had more to do to relieve the pressure on her mother. Kay could not just say, "I have things to do"; the excuse had to be a good one if she were not coming for the weekend. During that period of her life, Kay felt that if she did anything for herself, it would be "almost selfish"; when she bought new clothes she expected her mother to say that she was showing off. Kay did not tell anyone in the family what she was earning, explaining, "It would make my brother-in-law feel bad."

Up until the time the referral was made, nothing had changed. Kay did not get a baby-sitter so she could go out. None of her sisters had a baby-sitter just to have free time. They did not have the money, so Kay hid that she had the money. For the same reason, she did not have a cleaning woman either. Kay was "keeping the trust."

Kay also would have liked a larger house. But she could hear her mother saying, "What's the matter with this house?" Since Kay had not brought up the subject of a larger house, there was no way so far to know whether her mother would actually say this or not. In fact, Kay had done nothing recently that would test out how the others felt and whether there was actually any reason to continue keeping the trust. But Kay thought her mother would not want the other sisters to feel bad. "So let's not have havoc about my house."

The way Kay put it is the way we have heard many people put it: "I don't know why I don't get up and do something. I have had a lot of options. But something stops me from putting my hand out . . . I never functioned to my ability. I sabotage myself." Kay believed that she would not stop hurting till she developed her own life, but she did not know where to start. "I

don't know what I want to do when I grow up.'' This was some-
how tied to the feeling that her own interests were not important, that her energy must continue to go into the trust.

REWORKING KAY'S ENTITLEMENT

The converging efforts of the therapist and a career counselor
brought Kay's sense of entrapment into direct conflict with her
hopes for the future and created a turbulent passage in Kay's life.
The critical events of this passage occurred over a two-month
period that began with Kay's referral by the therapist to the career
counselor. From the therapist's point of view, as Kay struggled
with this issue, the sense of restraint within tight parameters
became as palpable as if she were actually throwing herself again
and again against a physical barrier.

After the initial session with the counselor, Kay reported to
her therapist that she felt like a dunce. She just did not know
what she wanted. The counseling session had left her feeling very
lonely, very empty, and very sorry for herself. The hour with the
counselor was unprecedented in Kay's life because it was an hour
spent with someone who devoted intense, undivided, and sym-
pathetic interest to the question of what kind of work Kay might
want to do. This was a sharp contrast with Kay's recent account
of past conversations with her mother. When Kay was working,
her mother would call up and ask how work was. Kay would
start to tell her and her mother would change the subject. For
Kay, the intervention of the counselor triggered an instant loyalty
crisis: How is it possible to admit that someone shows more interest than her mother has ever shown? This alone would be
enough to block Kay's responses and make her feel like a ''dunce.''

During her treatment hours, Kay made repeated attempts to
get at the childhood roots of her present inability. ''As a child
I was never heard, never listened to. They had the facts. I could
not compete with my father. Nobody cared about my opinion,
I didn't have one.'' Shifting to her present efforts at making a
breakthrough, Kay would observe, ''It's hard for me to say, 'I
just can't stay home.' It's hard because I don't have my reasons

for what I'm doing.'' An unyielding logic seemed to be at work here. Kay could not leave the house until she could justify it with a reason, and she had never been allowed to have a valid reason.

Making the connection between past and present, Kay also observed, ''What I have to do is never as important as what Jim wants. I'd have to take a monumental stand to say no. So it's the same as with my parents. It's getting clear.'' Clear, that is, that she needed always to be at someone else's beck and call, letting them set the terms solely according to what they wanted of her. She believed Jim just wanted her to go on being ''good old Kay.'' In her therapy sessions, Kay was sometimes gripped by the conviction that this was how things with Jim really were, a perception that was accompanied by severe distress, even agitation. At other moments, she would acknowledge that she knew Jim was not really the problem, and then her agitation would get worse, because this meant having to face the real source of the problem all over again.

The first session with the counselor had left Kay feeling like a ''dunce,'' and successive sessions seemed only to deepen this feeling. As part of a ''lifeline'' exercise, the counselor asked Kay to list the ten most important past achievements of her life, a request that brought Kay to the verge of panic. She told her therapist:

> This was the hardest of all the tests. It was really impossible for me, because it was like, I really had no achievements. So I kept putting it off and putting it off. And I didn't get it done. So we started working on what the word ''achievement'' meant, and I felt it had to be some kind of outstanding accomplishment. She wanted to know why I didn't think having my daughter was an achievement. I said, ''Everybody has kids, what's the big deal about having a child?'' I feel like I really had no achievements because things were just expected out of me and I did the normal thing. I never thought I did anything outstanding. It brought out the thing we were talking about, I never had any achievements because I was never allowed to be different from anybody else. Even when I ran that race where I won the trophy, I wasn't excited about it.

I wasn't expected to feel excited about it, and nobody else was going to feel excited about it.

Kay was not suffering because of any paucity of past achievement. What she had done was to take all her past experiences and fit them neatly within the parameters of her designated place by defining them as nonevents. If nobody else had any expectations about the event, then it was not infused with life, it was meaningless. If someone else *did* have an expectation of her, then she was only performing on cue and it was still meaningless.

During this period, Kay also clung to the conviction that her family's attitudes toward any new milestones in her life would be as uncompromising as ever. With another child on the way, for instance, she realized that she and Jim needed a bigger house, and after some argument they had agreed on a particular house that would fit their needs. But she believed her family would think she was crazy to buy it.

THE EFFORT TO BREAK THROUGH

Repeatedly during this period, the therapist and the career counselor sought to bring Kay into confrontation with what she had done that was good. The therapeutic task at this point could be defined as an effort to help her deal with the anxiety about family loyalties that was blocking an accurate perception of herself. During one session, the therapist returned to the topic of Kay's work with the investment banking service, and pressed her for further reactions. Kay seemed to find it hard to remember. ''I guess I was proud of it.'' The therapist asked Kay if she had told anybody about the job.

When I told my parents, it was like, I got this job, I don't think I told them to the extent of what I had to go through to get the job. I made light of it. I didn't brag to them, let's put it that way. You just didn't do that. You know, you had a pompous kind of a selfish feeling from doing something like that. I made it sound easy, I made the job sound easy, any donkey could do it.

Having thus classed herself with the donkey, it is not hard to see how Kay could more recently have classified herself as a dunce.

Only after she had entered her seventh month of weekly therapy sessions, and after weeks of encouragement from both her counselor and her therapist, could Kay bring herself to mention two of the most significant things about her banking service job. She had been the first woman to be employed by the company. And she had won awards for her sales records. As usual, she had succeeded in converting these to nonevents by assigning them to the category of simply doing the normal thing, doing what somebody else expected of her. Only now could she begin to reexamine these events for new meanings. She was able to relate to the therapist her new ability to distinguish between two kinds of sales calls she had made.

I don't consider just selling an achievement. But if the guy really resists and I persisted at it, and I get the sale, that's an achievement, like I'm almost daring myself to get this guy and I'll get him in the long run. It wasn't just for the money or anything like that, it was a personal achievement.

I'm almost daring myself. For the first time we heard an expression that came out of Kay's own search for a way to strive, to produce. By putting such an experience into words, she had taken a step outside the old parameters. But there was no way to take such a step without touching off a fresh round of anxiety. "I do get this feeling with this whole counseling thing that I'm looking for something I'm not going to find—can life really change, so I'm hanging on a kind of shoestring about that."

UPDATE WITH JIM

Seeing her relationship to Jim as hopeless had been one piece of Kay's legacy of hopelessness. As she struggled to change, her perception of him fluctuated between hope and recurring despair. The fluctuation was driven partly by her own shifting states of mind and partly by what was going on between Kay and Jim while she was struggling with change. During one therapy session, she described how let down she felt after attempting to share something about a career counseling session with Jim. When she got home from her session Jim was on the telephone, and by the time he finally remembered to ask her about it, "I had crashed. It's amazing how fast I came down. He missed my point. I felt tired, disappointed. I was so deflated. I can't rely on anybody, nobody cares what I'm doing." Whatever Jim had done or failed to do, it made Kay feel again as if she were talking to her mother. Jim and Kay still had a long way to go before there would be a sense that things could be freely shared.

Just as Jim had originally seemed dismayed at the prospect of how much he would have to change in order to repair the marriage, now it seemed as if he might be dismayed at the prospect that not everything was his fault. Kay observed that a new pattern had emerged and kept repeating itself. She would, as in the past, momentarily fly off the handle over something like his being late getting home. She would then recognize that the distress she was feeling at the moment had little to do with Jim. While she was realizing this, Jim was going through his customary effort to make amends for being late. He would then become disconcerted because his efforts did not seem to produce the desired result—Kay's mood did not bounce back to normal. Jim might then engage in more tortured efforts to make amends, or he might demand to know why Kay was not accepting his apology. Like many husbands, Jim was standing on the edge of an abyss, beginning to sense that there was a great deal going on with Kay that he had not caused, over which he really had very little control, and that might, if it got loose, intrude in all kinds of strange ways on their marriage. As Kay put it, "He wants to discuss the fifteen minutes late, he keeps going back to things he can control, touch . . . He's kind of lost, he knows there's something he has to do on his part, but he doesn't know what to do."

Nor did Kay, at this point, have a clear enough idea of what she did want from Jim to be able to tell him about it. Kay's image of Jim still reflected her old perception of her family and especially of her father, whose need for control of the family seemed limitless. Loyalty to the family had kept Kay from looking at the possibility that her husband might be a better man than her father, just as it had kept her from seeing that she had the capacity to outdo her father as well as her sisters and her brothers-in-law. But the times began to come more frequently when Jim and Kay could wiggle loose from her old perceptions, and as this happened Jim began to show at least partial relief and hopefulness about the marriage.

At the same time, however, another facet of the problem was inexorably thrusting itself forward: Kay was attempting to put more time into her work with her counselor, and Jim seemed to be raising objections. As Kay put it to him: ''This is the first time it's my project I'm working on, and you are taking away from it, with your, 'Yes, but we have to do so and so.''' Kay and Jim were beginning to pick up the cues that a change in her outlook on herself might involve very significant shifts in how her hours and her energies were allocated, but as a couple they had not yet begun to explore together what these shifts might be, let alone how they might be productively negotiated. It sounded to the therapist like an offer on Jim's part to begin explorations when he replied to Kay, ''I can understand a business word like 'project.'''

In the ensuing weeks, Kay and Jim worked hard at forging a ''team'' approach. They were elated when it worked, and, when it did not, they were afraid of ''slipping back into the pit.'' This meant, in effect, that if Jim seemed to Kay to be bent on opposing her, she might ''hammer him away'' and then they would have to start all over again. They had still not reached the point where each could trust the other to hear, and to respect, true differences of opinion or style, but they were on the way toward doing so. As Kay observed, ''Jim *can* help a lot when he knows he's not to blame.''

It was clear enough by now that movement with Jim was partially contingent on Kay's ability to gain new perspectives on the old family patterns that had led her to feel so frustrated about her own efforts. Most important was the reworking of her sense of entitlement, of what she had owed, did owe, and would owe to family. She could not simply turn her back on this question, because to do so would be to leave the invisible loyalty to the old way of doing things in place, in full force and effect. The ideal outcome would be to arrive at a new set of understandings with members of the family about what was to be given and received. To achieve this, Kay could initiate trial actions. If people responded, she could then take the next steps that were called for. If people did not respond, then the goal might have to be reduced, but at least Kay would have tried.

Kay was in fact initiating trial actions, with mixed feelings about the results. She reported that she had been able successfully to ask her mother to use the train for visits so that Kay would not have to make two round trips with the car. But when the therapist asked Kay what she felt the family expected of her, Kay seemed discouraged. "I feel kind of sad that now I just don't go out of my way the way I used to and I'm not sure they understand. If I don't go out of my way, it's kind of like, 'You seem really tired or down, are you depressed?'— and I just don't bother to explain myself."

Kay initiated attempts to tell two of her siblings what she was doing with the career counselor. Their initial reactions were well within the old parameters: "Well, you're crazy, now's the time you can spend with the kids." "Well, what about the kids?" Kay's old response to these comments would have been that their opinion outweighed hers and she was being selfish. Instead, as she put it, "I did feel I'm making a statement. I'm not just sitting here, I do have something." She went back to one of the siblings for a second try. Again, her sister's response was parameter-bound: "You think the family is unimportant." Her sister was concerned that if Kay ignored her children now, Kay would find herself alone in her old age. Kay was unable to explain to her sister how she was attempting to break through the old barrier between family and personal achievement. But Kay was at least able to feel that she had attempted to initiate a dialogue with her sisters. This open effort at loyalty would serve to take some of the force and effect out of the old, invisible loyalty. Kay's effort to initiate such a dialogue, whether it was successful or not, enabled Kay to feel that she had taken a step toward individuation and at the same time paid an appropriate amount on whatever her debt to her family might be.

By the end of the second month of her work with the career counselor, Kay found that the hysteria had gone out of her feelings about her present place in life.

> Right now I find that I really don't mind being alone. I'm kind of enjoying—the lack of hysteria, the quietness of not getting worked up. I'm trying to put together a concept of what is needed in a profession or whatever, looking for patterns from the past that will be needed to hook onto something from the future.

Accepting help from her counselor was no longer an act of disloyalty because, through her therapy, Kay was taking steps to make appropriate payment on whatever debt she still owed her family. The fact that Kay's career efforts had not yet produced specific results was no longer a source of distress, nor was the fact that she and Jim still had a long way to go. For now, Kay could feel at peace and later look back on this moment as a milestone.

12

The Team Approach

Career issues are often more relevant to family therapy than might be expected and so deserve more attention than they are usually given. At the same time, when an issue of job change or career movement arises, therapists need to recognize the possibility that a referral is appropriate.

In reality, there are times when career counseling begins to take on aspects of therapy and times when therapy takes on aspects of career counseling, and when the lines are hazy the question becomes, who should handle what? The ideal approach would be with a team made up of a career counselor and a family therapist, but creating such a team might not be as easy as it sounds, especially in sections of the country where professionals are isolated. Career counselors do not always have access to compatible family therapists, and family therapists may not know of informed career counselors. And few career counselors have exposed themselves to family systems theory, so the two do not usually speak the same language.

In the first chapter, Mark created an effective team by detriangling himself and forcing his therapist and career counselor to work together. In the last chapter, Kay was more fortunate in that she had a therapist who maintained a solid working relationship with a career counselor and made a referral at the appropriate time.

The following case involves a client who could not afford both therapy and career counseling but who was lucky enough to find a counselor with training in family systems. The case was presented to the authors by the counselor, and after the presentation the authors interviewed the counselor to look at similarities and differences of approach.

THE CASE OF ROBIN

Robin was a 31-year-old woman who was still living at home with her parents when she came for counseling. She wanted help because she had been unable to stick with a job for more than six months at a time.

After high school, her educational record was as spotty as her work history. She had dropped out of college a couple of times, until she finally went to work full time and finished an art degree by attending college in the evenings. She had artistic talent but had never used it in her work, always taking jobs instead as a bookkeeper or a secretary. She was significantly overweight when she began counseling and at the time she was continuing to gain weight. She seemed very depressed.

Her family was poor and her mother had to work. But it had not always been that way, a fact that emerged from her written autobiography. She was born into an exceedingly wealthy family for whom prosperity was, at the time, in its second generation. Her mother's family had been prosperous all her life, and Robin's father had been given a place in his wife's family business. Robin remembers that her father enjoyed the status and prosperity of the business but did not seem to have any real responsibilities there. Robin grew up with maids and butlers, but she remembers little contact with her parents when she was young because they socialized so actively. She had no responsibilities, and the only things that were required of her were that she wash her face and brush her teeth. She had no chores of any kind, and she had a great deal of free time to play and draw and dance.

Robin did well in school but at first she had difficulty social-izing, and she tended to move off by herself. Learning to read, she said, allowed her to escape into a fantasy world where she was happier.

As Robin moved through middle childhood, it was clear to her that her father was not measuring up to the standards set by his in-laws. His lack of status and responsibility at work had gen-erated a lethargy that was now apparent in all aspects of family life. Robin's maternal grandparents made it clear they felt their daughter had married below her station in life, and over the years this attitude became a self-fulfilling prophecy that eventually began to undermine the marriage, the family, and the family business.

Robin came to love school, became a champion swimmer and an accomplished dancer, and eventually developed close friend-ships there. But when she was nine her family moved to another town and after the move she experienced her first academic dif-ficulties. When she was 11 she became attached to a male teacher, who sparked her creativity and renewed her interest in learning, but was fired that year because of his antiwar activities. Once again her performance declined. She seemed to be particularly vulnerable to this loss, probably because she had no real rela-tionship with her father, who at this stage seemed to be a weak, hazy character, passive, unassertive, and probably badly depressed. Robin had a difficult time generating many memories of him from this stage in her life, although she expressed no current or re-collected sense of loss where her father was concerned. The teacher who was fired was the first adult male she connected with, and any sense of loss she remembers is attached to him.

Around this time Robin's maternal grandparents retired and turned the family business over to Robin's father, who ran it into the ground in less than a year and caused the family to have to move once again. Her father started a new company but it folded, too. Ever since that time he has moved in and out of various jobs and ventures, none of which ever succeeded. The family lived on her mother's family money until it was gone, at which point her mother was forced to go to work as a secretary. This happened about three years before Robin came for counseling.

Robin's parents played her against one another from the time she was 11 or 12, especially when financial difficulties put added stress on the marriage. This continued until Robin finally escaped to college in the Midwest when she was 19. She reported that she was happy and successful at college until the middle of her sophomore year, when her mother showed up on campus one day to tell her that if she was going to attend college at all she would have to do it closer to home.

It turned out that Robin's younger brother had just run away and Robin's parents seemed unable to tolerate the empty nest. Family problems had escalated significantly during the time Robin had been away at college and the stress and conflict she found waiting for her were overwhelming. She went back to college, but not with her former enthusiasm and academic success, and after a few months she dropped out to take a job as a secretary. After a few more months, terribly dissatisfied with herself, she quit work and went back to school once again, but within a month of that move discovered that she was pregnant. She ran away from home, only to have her mother find her and bring her back again. She considered keeping the baby but her mother insisted on an abortion. She got another job and went to college part time, eventually finishing her degree with a major in art, but she took no joy or sense of accomplishment from her work or from the college degree.

When counseling began, Robin had been out of work for almost a year. She was still the pivotal member of her family, and her mother and father communicated with each other only through her. Understandably, each attempt she made to go out on her own had been undermined, sometimes by her, sometimes by one of her parents. Conflicts between Robin's parents, or sometimes between Robin and her father, had recently turned violent, and on several occasions her father had broken down the door to her bedroom after she had gone there to escape an argument.

Robin's test results reemphasized her talent in art and her high level of creativity. But it took nearly four months of counseling before she gained enough confidence to even start looking for work in fields where creativity and artistic talent might be applied. When she interviewed she received positive feedback on her talent, energy, and self-presentation. People said she came across as articulate, well-read, and confident, but she never felt good about the interviews and always found ways to undermine the reasons for the positive feedback.

Her mother would clip ads for secretarial or bookkeeping jobs from the local paper, but when Robin began to talk about calling to apply, her father would make critical comments about the job, the company, or Robin's limitations. On two occasions during counseling, when Robin was considering a career move into the art field, her parents made contact with the counselor to complain that the counselor was encouraging Robin to go beyond her limits by trying to force her into a career area that would be over her head or a waste of her time. "Why don't you just tell her to be happy with being a secretary?" the mother demanded.

It seemed that if Robin became any more successful than either of her parents she would be more likely to leave home, an event that was feared by everyone concerned, including Robin. So no direct confrontation with the fusion that held Robin in place was attempted and instead the emphasis was placed on Robin's right to hold a job that she found personally rewarding and meaningful. Before Robin could be free enough to do this, however, her sense of herself as a loyal member of a family of failures had to be addressed, and an autobiographical narrative and a "life inventory summary" were used to spotlight these entitlement issues.

Through long talks about what she felt her family obligations were and how she might be able to balance these with obligations to herself, Robin began to see that she might be able to manage both her family role and a meaningful career. Fantasy was used to generate scripts for role play, and later, for actual use during real interviews.

Robin was encouraged to go the informal route in her job

search by networking—developing contacts in the art field through friends, associates, teachers, and fellow students. She had a limited number of friends at this point, and the networking process helped increase her social contacts. It also finally paid off with a job offer, and after four months of interviewing, Robin became an associate art director for a small publishing company. The job did not exist when she went to interview with the company, but the publisher was so impressed with her that he created the slot.

It was clear from the start that Robin was being groomed to replace the art director when he retired, and she was successful enough in her performance to become art director after a little more than a year. During that time she started to take off weight, and now reports that she looks just like she did when she first went to college. She continues to live at home.

INTERVIEW

Dunne: We'll come back to Robin in a second, but to get our interview off the ground, could we start with a description, in a phrase or two, of what a traditional career counselor does?

Career Counselor: Well, in general, I think of the career counselor, myself included, as a coach who helps people assess themselves, set realistic career goals and then develop and implement a strategy to meet those goals.

Ulrich: How did you get interested in family systems theory?

Career Counselor: Mostly through my own therapy and then workshops, seminars, readings, tapes on Bowen, Nagy, Haley, Minuchin, Fogarty, McGoldrick, Ackerman, and so on.

Dunne: Would you say that this background separates you from the traditional career counselor?

Career Counselor: Yes. It takes me deeper into the personal issues that have an impact on a person's career choices.

Ulrich: How has it helped to incorporate a family systems awareness?

Career Counselor: The first thing that comes to mind is that it helps me give people solid evidence that real change is possible. People come for counseling in crisis, and it soon becomes clear that they have been repeating patterns of behavior that work against them as they move from job to job or even within the same job. So at some level people feel that change is not possible. They feel stuck. Some traditional counselors don't attempt to address that stuckness or to intervene in repetitious self-defeating patterns. Issues of that nature take them too deep into the personality and too close to raw emotion. It helps me to recognize that the source of that stuckness is usually in the family system, maybe because, in a way, it makes me more comfortable with emotion. But still, I'm not a therapist. I'm not afraid to deal with emotion, and clients frequently weep with me over the ways they've been restricted by their family or as they realize how they've restricted themselves. I'll sit with someone who is crying but I won't ask why the tears. I will be compassionate and let them cry and often encourage them to explore their feelings with someone they feel comfortable with. Or I may, at the appropriate time, suggest that they see a therapist.

Dunne: How did your family systems training help you with Robin?

Career Counselor: Robin was generally undifferentiated, as shown by her introvert-extrovert scale on the Myers Briggs. It's easy to see how stuck in her family system she is and to acknowledge that she will not be free to be herself in a career or in relationships until she gets unstuck. So we moved to free her as much as possible in the career area. When counseling terminated, she was still living at home, but she had gone into therapy, with the expressed goal of developing the courage to move out of the house.

Ulrich: She'll probably have to persuade her therapist to take her place in the family.

Career Counselor: Her feeling is, and I think she's right, that when she leaves, her parents won't have anybody to stand between them, and whether or not they can deal with their issues without a buffer remains to be seen. Up till now, the ties in this family have been so tight that Robin hasn't had the courage yet to deal with the issue of separation. She had to become self-sufficient first, while still living up to what she feels as her family obligation.

Dunne: I think any therapist would support the notion that her career steps were steps toward differentiation. It's interesting how much your case presentation sounded like a case a family therapist might present. But your methods of eliciting family material are different. And so are the ways you make use of the family material.

Career Counselor: The main difference is the work focus. I have clients write a detailed work autobiography, going back as far as possible to look at, first, the importance of work in the family: What did mother and father do and how did they seem to feel about work? What kind of emphasis did the family place on work and work-related values? Then I ask about various life stages; for example, "Up to five or six years old, what do you remember as being work; what did you have to do because your parents told you to do it, that you just didn't do because you were playing?" And then the early school years, until about 11: "What was your approach to school work, to learning, to family chores, to any work-related activities outside of school or the family?" And then the junior high years, with the first paid jobs. Then the rest of the teen years and the college years, but always keeping an eye on what was happening with the family, both in general family systems terms but especially in terms of work, with career changes, family moves, changes of status and earning. I also explore attitudes, feelings, sources of motivation and satisfaction as well as money.

Dunne: But you don't plan interventions aimed at the family system? And you don't teach systems theory to your clients?

Career Counselor: I tell people that I don't get into the "whys" of things. I look at this family background material as the given or source of a situation. And from there we can look at the degree to which these issues or themes or dynamics get acted out inappropriately in the work setting. Someone bright like Robin could see without being pushed how she chose work situations where she would not be as successful as she might have wanted her father to be, or where the authority figure was violent, at least violent verbally, like father. And as these themes emerged we would talk about them, but always in the context of career. Overall, I stick with the work theme, and if family dynamics fall into place around it, then we work with them.

Dunne: It sounds as if your approach has more in common with psychotherapies that use increased awareness as their primary leverage, not with those that use intervention techniques within the systemic structure.

Career Counselor: Increased awareness combined with assertiveness training intervention aimed at behavior modification. Until you enable a client to identify behaviors that are not working in their best interest, it's very difficult for them to make changes in any area. It goes along with the idea behind assertiveness training, that if you practice new behaviors and get positive feedback, this will enable change to take place. But until you understand the family systems issues, you can't as effectively coach people to change because you won't understand the forces that hold the client in place or that rise up to work against change once it begins. But with this in mind, I'll teach people new behaviors, new skills for interviewing or for dealing with a boss or subordinate, based on assertiveness training techniques, and frequently these end up being applied in the family.

Ulrich: If I were working with Robin in therapy, what I'd probably be doing at this point, once we had established that she was restricting herself based on her role in her family, would be to go back to family of origin issues and do a lot of work on her entitlement.

Dunne: And that's where the two approaches seem to part company.

Career Counselor: Exactly. What I do at that point instead is to bring the testing data in so that we can be objective about character, personality, and motivational issues. We address these, but without a therapeutic slant, always with a career focus, always bringing it back to motivation, interest, decision-making. For example, one of the inventories measured Robin's passivity, but the only use I made of that was to point out how she'll have to be careful in terms of proceeding into and through work situations, how it might undermine her and why. I try to emphasize the positive feedback to show that clients have the innate ability to change and that they can use the best parts of themselves for themselves. Often clients will recognize that they have strong skills in various areas such as communication, organization, persuasion, and analysis. However, they do not recognize that they can use these skills for themselves to better their situation in general, as well as for future employment.

Ulrich: Another way of characterizing what you're doing is that you are providing tools that give the client some leverage to use on her designation to open up a range of choice. In a way, the skill assessment techniques can be used as leverage against the designation.

Career Counselor: Right. Family issues like that show up in my values exercises. Themes of achievement, recognition, knowledge, self-worth emerge as primary motivating factors that seem to be imparted by the family. Sometimes these are inherited values and not ones the person would consciously accept for themselves, given the choice.

Ulrich: It's also evident from your work that you have an appreciation for family loyalty and the power of legacy. At least you didn't push against the tide with Robin. And you didn't make the mistake so many make, of telling Robin that she is stuck because she has crazy people for parents.

Dunne: And of course if there's anything to the business of interlocking systems, an intervention—or a behavior modification—used in the work system should have a spillover effect in the family. An intervention in one system becomes an intervention in the other.

Ulrich: Provided it's not done with a crowbar.

Career Counselor: I see that spillover effect all the time. With

Robin, when we were talking about how to network, how to present herself to people, we worked on a script designed to let Robin present herself as she was, not as she thought her parents wanted her to be and not as the ideal person she could never be. We role-played as we developed the script and then she went and tried it out. And the response was so positive as she used her script with people, some she didn't even know, that she decided to try it with her father. This was how she was finally able to say to her father, "Look, I'm doing this job hunt the way I want to do it and I want you to leave me alone." For Robin, that was a gigantic step.

Dunne: To play devil's advocate for a second. A hard-nosed clinician might say you had no business taking on this case in the first place, that as soon as you heard some of the background you should have made a referral to therapy. Some might go a step further and suggest that by looking only at those symptoms that showed up in job-related issues, you were joining the system that was exploiting this woman's inabilities so as to keep from ever facing deeper issues in the family.

Career Counselor: I couldn't agree more. But Robin had no money and was out of work. We spoke of her need for therapy but we agreed that the first step was to get a job, one that would be a positive experience for her, and then to seek therapy, which is the way it worked it out. You have to address the person where they are when they come for help and you use what leverage you have. And the reality is that people are moving in and out of various systems all the time. So you plug in based on your reading of the client's primary need, and you work carefully because you know that efforts made in one area are going to cause change in other areas as well. This is something everyone has to realize.

Ulrich: It's a new awareness for many psychotherapists, too, that they are responsible for the impact of their work on a wide circle of people where a client's changes will cause change. At the same time, it would be a mistake to give the impression that family therapy can be done simply by working with someone's work issues.

Dunne: Still, I wonder if more couldn't be done in the context of career counseling based on systems thinking, especially when a client's family legacy is so very restricting the way it was for Robin. In this case, rather than have Robin bucking her family legacy, either being a prisoner of it and then, as a result of your counseling, coming to hate it or hate her parents—or distance herself only to get pulled back—you wisely neutralized its impact on Robin's career by building her self-worth in that one area. But the more successful she is, the more we can expect the family system to tighten its hold on her in other areas. So I'm wondering if something more aggressive could have been done to harness the power of her legacy and her family system and force these to work for her, perhaps paradoxically. Without thinking it out, for instance, what if you were to suggest that since she's already making a career out of her role as daughter, she ought to demand that her parents pay her a reasonable salary?

Career Counselor: That begins to seem like therapy. The focus shifts away from work, and we start talking more about her family and less about her career. When that happens, the specific goal of career growth can get lost. The process of working through all those family issues isn't part of the contract I establish. For my work, where family legacy is concerned, I find that two things happen: either there's the giving in to legacy, being dominated by it, or there's a rebellion against it, and both positions are counterproductive and enervating for the person. Growth in the career area, a developing entitlement, helps separate the person from either of those poles. So we work to get clients to begin to define themselves on their own terms in the career area, which seems to be an area of life that most people can readily claim as their own, even if they've been giving a lot away to their parents on an unconscious level.

Ulrich: It's established that work is one of the factors that contributes to individuation, but you could go a step further to say that the process of separating one's working life from that of one's parents, or from the designations of the family, is perhaps the very crux of individuation, especially since it usually comes at a critical point, when a collision with the legacy is apt to occur.

Career Counselor: The self-assessment component of the career counseling, including the autobiography, the accomplishment and skill assessment, and values clarification exercises, is geared toward that individuating process. For some people it's the first time they step back and look at themselves from a separate position. The exercises themselves start the process moving. After that, it's a matter of coaching a person through a variety of experiences aimed at modifying identified patterns of behavior, which are based more often than not on legacy and on old tapes from the family system. Once a person identifies patterns and looks at the behaviors involved, they can begin to change. I focus on the behavior itself—through role playing, scripting, fantasy work with guided imagery, journal work—but when someone's in therapy at the same time it's absolutely a marvelous and powerful experience because they're able to deal with the "whys" of the situation, which I don't go into, while they're trying on new behaviors that alter their old patterns. I also encourage clients to talk over with the therapist what they are doing with me. Also, I will communicate with the therapist, but only after discussing it with the clients.

Ulrich: We're talking about themes that go beyond work-related issues and reach into matters of personality, status, ego, self-worth. That's why a team approach is so very important.

Career Counselor: That's certainly true. The career work goes much faster and smoother if family therapy is taking place at the same time, especially if it can be coordinated, especially when the client is facing issues of separation the way Robin was.

Dunne: Okay, but it may not always be possible to create the team approach. And aren't we, between the lines of our book,

telling family therapists that they should increase their awareness and skills in career and workplace issues?

Career Counselor: I'd hate to see you give the impression that by
learning a few of the career counselor's techniques, the
therapist can incorporate career counseling with psychotherapy. So many therapists have never set foot in the business
world and don't know what they're talking about when they
address work issues. I'd also hate to see career counseling
become a subset of psychotherapy or family therapy the way
marital therapy is. I think it is critically important for therapists and career counselors to find each other and begin
to communicate and work with each other. It can also be
a resource for mutual referral.

Ulrich: I suppose our book is saying something to career counselors, too, that since their methods tap into such rich family
material they owe it to themselves and their clients to catch
up with family systems thinking. It cuts both ways. Seen in
this light, family issues provide new leverage for the counselor the same way work or career issues become another
door therapists can open to encounter the family system.

13

Conclusions

To a greater extent than has been acknowledged, motivations of people at work come from the deeply ingrained patterns originating in the family system. We believe these patterns have tended to go unrecognized, and their effects when recognized have tended to be minimized, as the result of two interacting myths.

One of these myths is that everything that happens in business is rational. A careful observer soon realizes that this is unsound and misleading. For instance, it appears that many managers seek by various strategies to *slow down* the output of their subordinates in order to prevent innovative upstarts from taking over power too soon, a pattern reflecting parents' fears of becoming obsolete and replaced by their children. Businesses abound with such patterns of behavior that do not fit the rational goals of the business.

The other myth can be stated as a legacy: it is the legacy of our society that we are not bound by legacies, that we as individuals set our own limits, as if each of us were totally free agents. We often dismiss as lapses of individual nerve what in fact may be the result of legacies dictating what we are or are not permitted to do, such legacies exerting all the more effect because they do their work invisibly.

Family patterns exert their influence in a multitude of ways. First, individuals relate their sense of security in the most basic way to the place they occupy in the family. This place is a designated place, the designation itself woven out of a multitude of strands. It includes what the rest of the family *perceive to be* the capacities and characteristics of the person, and so it can be directly affected by the present narcissistic needs of other family members. It is profoundly affected by the legacies of previous generations. Such legacies may contain general terms for the whole family; e.g., this family is to keep a low profile. Or the terms may be specific to the individual; e.g., the oldest son is the only one who is to succeed. Almost from the first days of life, tension begins to develop between the self-directed efforts of the individual and the family's admonitions, which are based on the individual's newly forming designation. Of course, this process of socialization is what makes the individual capable of coexisting with others; but it can take place only within the confines of what other family members perceive, and thus, allow, based on their present needs and past learnings. Even if the individual makes forceful efforts to resist, the designation may be binding due to the holding power not only of love for other family members but also of loyalty to the family, which is all the more powerful when it operates unseen.

The designation defining the individual's place in the family is based on not only how the individual relates to other family members, but also how the individual fits into other family members' relationships to one another. A child who is exposed to fighting parents gradually may assume the role of peacemaker, and this may become the central theme of his or her designation. Thus the patterns are ones that involve the person with two or more other members of the family. The concept of one-to-one transference is inadequate to convey what it means to relate, not simply to one person or another, *but to what is going on between those other persons.* When this pattern of relating is carried into the workplace, a *systemic* transference is taking place; i.e., the transference elements have to do with one's part in a system, not merely with one other person. Thus an individual whose parents fought and was afraid they might turn and make him the scapegoat may be terrified when superiors at work fight over anything in which he has played even the slightest part.

Another significant way in which family patterns exert their influence at work is through relationships with co-workers who, of course, also bring their designated patterns of behavior with them. Family therapists are by now familiar with the uncanny dovetailing of relational patterns that occurs with married couples; it often seems that each must have unconsciously sought out the one other person in the whole world who could provide the most stress at all of his or her sorest points. A similar process appears to occur at work. Either because it is not so uncommon for people with complementary patterns to be juxtaposed to each other, or because they tend to seek each other out, it does not seem hard to find actors at work who will stand in for the absent family members and, through their behavior, reinforce whatever patterns an individual has brought along from home. Thus, a woman with a clinging and sadistic mother and a passive father may be overwhelmed when she encounters a clinging, sadistic female supervisor whose own boss seems to condone what is happening. Each worker then engages in transference and is simultaneously part of others' transferences.

The workplace also is ready to duplicate the home scene in a broader sense. Not only are there actors waiting to play the family parts, but also, the whole pattern of behavior and of emotional process at work has much in common with what happens in the family. Of course, the workplace is oriented to rational goals, but it is run and maintained by people, so no matter how hard organizational experts try to provide rational guidelines for work behavior, the human element tends to be a more powerful influence on what actually goes on.

It is important to the individual to recognize that a business is not just like a family. Failure to grasp this crucial distinction can lead to embarrassing setbacks; it can even interfere with a person's movement toward individuation. But recognizing similar patterns is also crucial if one is to grasp what is going on within the organization.

The vertical hierarchy of the organization provides the basic template to which the family patterns can be applied. Attitudes toward previous generations in the family can be transferred to one's superiors at work. The vertical stresses of the family, i.e., those occurring between generations, can compound the vertical stresses at work, i.e., those occurring between levels of the organization. The tendency of large organizations to build new layers of management plays into this process. The vertical stresses interact with the horizontal stresses, i.e., those having to do with the here and now, such as how to adapt manufacturing processes to new designs.

We suggest that the essence of productivity, the adaptation of existing resources to new ideas, is based in the here and now, and while the vertical hierarchy is indispensable, the stresses associated with it tend to get in the way of productivity. In business, as in the family, stresses tend to generate defensive behaviors. Looking at the individual who gets caught in organizational stress, we can see the resulting defenses such as avoidance, denial, isolation, projection of blame and badness, etc., the same maladaptive behaviors the individual probably employed when dealing with stress within the family system. From the point of view of family process, we see within organizations massive defensive operations taking place that resemble those occurring within a family, such as rigidity and the burying of individual initiatives for which no one is willing to be accountable.

The process is richly complicated by the fact that business hierarchies, like family hierarchies, lend themselves readily to a certain type of transaction, i.e., the formation of triangles. We know of the pernicious effects that can occur when family members lock themselves into triangles; individuals can just as readily slip into the same kinds of straitjackets at work. But the process of triangulation has broader effects at work, because the behavior of people who are locked into triangles at work tends to facilitate the transmission of anxiety downwards in the organization and to block the transmission of vital data upwards. Learning how to stay out of triangles and thereby free people to function is a skill that is in very great contrast to the efforts at manipulation of human resources practiced by many organizational experts, whose interventions often serve only to add to the power of the triangles. For example, the thrust of much work in "human resources" is to position the manager as an agent of those above in taking unilateral actions to modify the performance of those below, rather than as a person capable of productive, albeit authoritative, exchanges with co-workers. We consider it no accident that the peer group has been identified as a source of productivity at work because the peer group has no parallel in vertical family process, hence it does not provide hooks on which people can get snagged. The closest thing in families to a peer group is the husband-wife team, whose members are, of course, in a position to function as a peer group, rather than as superior and subordinate, if they are both willing to do so.

In shifting the focus from the organization back to the individual, we can see how work provides critical leverage for individuation, since in our culture, what one does is usually the barometer of this process. But individuation has, we believe, levels of complexity that have not been sufficiently recognized up to now. The individual tends to get tangled in three sometimes-conflicting sets of criteria, and the result can be a great deal of uncertainty about the self, especially about what is real and what is fake. The first set of criteria is the family designation: to succeed or fail, to be family caretaker, to keep a low profile, to avoid being an artist, teacher, or blue-collar worker, etc. The second set of criteria is provided at work: what one is expected to do in order to serve the company and thereby succeed. The third set of criteria deals with what is going on inside the self, the emerging sense of one's own interests and capacities. This can be quite confusing for the individual whose family has already dictated what his or her accomplishments are to be; for instance, a child may be caught up in the mother's fantasy that he or she is to become a great musician. Conversely, it may be confusing for the individual picked out for failure by the family but who has developed compensatory fantasies such as being a great musician. But most people are able to get at least some glimpses of what they as individuals, not merely as family members or organizational members, can and want to do.

Profound complications can arise if the person who is pursuing work and/or self criteria feels disloyal to the family designation. If the sense imbued by the family concerning what is real is at odds with what one has chosen for one's self, and one's loyalty to the family is strong enough so this sense cannot be thrown off, then one may feel unreal, a fake, in pursuing goals that the family did not mandate.

Of course, complications also can arise if the person who pursues family and/or work criteria feels that he or she is being disloyal to the self; and there are also well-recognized difficulties when one fails to achieve at the level of one's perfectionistic demands of self. But these are likely to be experienced as a conscious disappointment about one's lack of achievement, whereas the sense of unreality that comes from violating family mandates can make one doubt the essential validity of the self.

In line with the observations of Boszormenyi-Nagy, we believe that the binding force of family designation results in a situation of family loyalty in which children feel they owe an infinite debt to the family that must be paid off before they can claim any entitlement, permission, or authority to function effectively on their own. The situation is made worse when the parents make demands of the child and yet withhold acknowledgment of what he or she has done to meet those demands. As the child grows up and reaches middle age, uncertainties about what he or she has accomplished may be exacerbated if the parents are still incapable of recognizing or acknowledging what he or she has become. Lack of a valid sense of entitlement, of course, can have a profound impact upon self-esteem; the unconscious conviction that "I am not allowed to" is consciously experienced as "I am not good enough to."

While individuation may hinge on what one does, the broader task of individuation is one of balancing. If the process is to be fully successful, the balancing must proceed simultaneously on several fronts. In regard to work choice, one may at least attempt to find some integration of what the family wants, what the available employers want, and one's own preferences. Between work and other aspects of life, there are many balancing tasks to be performed because life does not provide an automatic "goodness of fit'' between individual life cycles or between individual and family life cycles. For instance, parents, peers, and society may expect a person to have arrived at a mature career choice when the person has not yet had time to acquire enough experience to make this choice possible. Or the marital partners' need for all-out commitment to their work in order to secure advancement may clash with the need to manage a pregnancy or take care of the children. Unless each partner is working to keep things in balance, each may feel entitled, by virtue of being drained at work, to put the domestic burden on the other. The efforts at balancing cannot be performed solo; they require skills in intrafamily negotiation, a group process aimed at a fair resolution of issues.

But the task of balancing involves dealing with major impediments: the displacement process, i.e., displacement of emotional conflict from work to home, can occur so quickly and unexpectedly that, for instance, a spouse who is enraged by a setback at work may not consciously experience this rage until he or she explodes at home when triggered by the other spouse who has failed to clean the house, discipline the children, or be a good lover. As long as the displacement intrudes, it may be impossible for any meaningful negotiations to proceed.

The balancing task also may be profoundly impeded, of course, by the intrusion of past designations. If one feels compelled by virtue of family designation to be the weak one, the strong one, or the wet blanket, then even the most heroic efforts at balancing of roles may continually collapse.

As we review these issues, it becomes evident that therapy may have a part to play in getting the individuation process and the process of negotiation between family members unstuck, by addressing not only the displacements but the underlying patterns of designated behavior and their associated emotional patterns. Again in line with the observations of Boszormenyi-Nagy, we believe that the key to effective release from the old claims of designation can be found, paradoxically, through the process of making adequate acknowledgment to one's origins. As a footnote to the case of Edith in Chapter 3 (p. 43), for instance, we can report that she was willing to engage for months in the patient exploration of any positive aspects that may have underlain the overwhelmingly negative mandate she received from her parents. The therapist pushed this pursuit along, even asking such questions as, ''Are you quite sure neither of your parents ever put a flower in your hair?'' This unabashedly sentimental question led to the memory that her mother had taken care to dress Edith prettily, and this in turn led Edith to recall that her mother made a big point of doing one's exercises, and thus a synergistic linkage emerged between mother's efforts and Edith's later success as a teacher of aerobics. Finding positive links like this between present and past relieves the client's need to keep engaging in unconscious, self-defeating acts of loyalty, and makes it easier to release for full and joyful use in the present the energies that had been bound up in the past. This is quite a different kind of therapy from merely helping the client to identify and thereby to ''throw off'' old bonds. We believe that this process may be, in some but not all cases, a necessary precursor to getting an individual moving, not only on the career path but also on the related path of successful negotiations with other family members to keep life in balance.

Comparing notes with a sensitive career counselor led us to the realization that identifying self-defeating patterns left over from the family may be as essential to career counseling as it is to therapy. Without overstepping the bounds of career counseling into the realm of therapy, the career counselor can use the work on choice and pursuit of career as leverage to help the individual move beyond designated roles. When this leverage alone is insufficient, the counselor may wish to enlist the services of the therapist. In therapy, when progress is blocked because the client possesses inadequate knowledge of career potential, either the potential within the self or the potential existing in the career world, then the therapist may need to enlist the services of the career counselor. This is in accord with our basic view that issues concerning work deserve to be regarded as one of the central issues of the therapeutic process.

References

Bernstein, P. (1985). *Family ties, corporate bonds*. New York: Doubleday.

Boszormenyi-Nagy, I. & Spark, G. (1973). *Invisible loyalties: Reciprocity in inter-generational family therapy*. New York: Harper & Row.

Boszormenyi-Nagy, I. & Ulrich, D. (1981). Contextual family therapy. In A. Gurman & D. Kniskern (Eds.), *Handbook of family therapy*. New York: Brunner/Mazel.

Bowen, M. (1978). *Family therapy in clinical practice*. New York: Jason Aronson.

deVries, M. (1984). Managers can drive their subordinates mad. In M. deVries (Ed.), *The irrational executive: Psychoanalytic explorations in management*. New York: International Universities Press.

deVries, M. & Miller, D. (1984). Unstable at the top. *Psychology Today, 18*, 26–34.

Day, M. (1985). Dual career marriages—making them work. *Harvard Business School Bulletin, 61*, 58–69.

Drucker, P. (1974). *Management: Tasks, responsibilities, practices*. New York: Harper & Row.

Erikson, E. (1950). *Childhood and society*. New York: Norton.

Erikson, E. (1968). *Identity, youth, and crisis*. New York: Norton.

LaBier, D. (1984). Irrational behavior in bureaucracy. In M. deVries (Ed.), *The irrational executive: Psychoanalytic explorations in management*. New York: International Universities Press.

Lawrence, P. & Lorsch, J. (1969). *Developing organizations: Diagnosis and action*. Reading: Addison-Wesley.

Levinson, D. (1978). *The seasons of a man's life*. New York: Alfred A. Knopf.

Mahler, S. (1979). *The selected papers of Margaret S. Mahler*. New York: Jason Aronson.

McGoldrick, M. & Carter, E. (1982). The family life cycle. In N. Walsh (Ed.), *Normal family processes*. New York: Guilford Press.

McLean, A. (1979). *Work stress*. Reading: Addison-Wesley.

Naisbitt, J. (1982). *Megatrends: Ten new directions transforming our lives*. New York: Warner Books.

Peters, T. & Waterman, Jr., R. (1982). *In search of excellence*. New York: Harper & Row.

Piotrkowski, C. (1979). *Work and the family system*. New York: Free Press.

Portner, J. (1983). Work and family: Achieving a balance. In H. McCubbin & C. Figley (Eds.), *Stress and the family* (Vol. 1). New York: Brunner/Mazel.

Schein, E. (1978). *Career dynamics: Matching individual and organizational needs*. Reading: Addison-Wesley.

Slipp, S. (1984). *Object relations: A dynamic bridge between individual and family treatment*. New York: Jason Aronson.

Sperry, B., Staver, N., Reiner, B., & Ulrich, D. (1954). Renunciation and denial in learning difficulties. *American Journal of Orthopsychiatry, 14*, 345–348.

Stierlin, H., Rucker-Embden, I., Wetzel, N., & Wirsching, M. (1980). *The first interview with the family*. New York: Brunner/Mazel.

Super, D. (1985). Coming of age in middletown: Careers in the making. *American Psychologist, 40*, 405–414.

Ulrich, D., Booz, D., & Lawrence, P. (1950). *Management behavior and foreman attitude: A case study*. Boston: Harvard Business School.

Wetzel, J. (1984). *Clinical handbook of depression*. New York: Gardner Press.

Wiseman, K. (1982). Emotional process in organizations. In R. Sagar, & K. Wiseman (Eds.), *Understanding organizations: Applications of family systems theory*. Washington: Georgetown University Family Center.

Index